Lions of England

Lions of England

A pictorial history of the King's Own Royal Regiment (Lancaster), 1680–1980

Stuart A. Eastwood

Keeper of Military History
Lancaster City Museum

SLP

Silver Link Publishing Ltd

This book is dedicated to all ranks past and present who
have served in the 4th King's Own.

To those, who in the days of old,
did not enrich themselves with gold,
but did their utmost to maintain
in Peace and War, the Regiment's name.
Anon

First published in November 1991

British Library Cataloguing in Publication Data

Eastwood, Stuart A.
Lions of England: a pictorial history of the King's
Own Royal Regiment (Lancaster), 1680–1980.
I. Title
356.110941

ISBN 0-947971-68-8

Silver Link Publishing Ltd
The Trundle
Ringstead Road
Great Addington
Kettering
Northants NN14 4BW

Typeset by Harper Phototypesetters Limited, Northampton
Printed in Great Britain by
Woolnough Bookbinding Limited, Irthlingborough, Northants,
and bound by The Bath Press, Bath

CONTENTS

**Title page The Regimental Depot, Bowerham Barracks,
Lancaster, c1933.**

FOREWORD

by Major-General Nigel St G. Gribbon OBE

The history of The King's Own Royal Regiment (Lancaster), contained in three volumes, written and edited by Colonels L. I. Cowper OBE and J. M. Cowper TD (WRAC), is acknowledged as one of the best documented histories in the British Army. There have also been other potted histories written by officers of the Regiment and numerous historical articles published in the Regimental Magazine, *The Lion and The Rose*, over many years. However, in this book Stuart Eastwood, Curator of the King's Own Museum, housed within Lancaster City Museum, has provided an entirely new and innovative work: a pictorial history, supported by historical summaries, covering the nine major epochs of the Regiment from its formation in 1680 for service in Tangier, to its amalgamation with the Border Regiment in 1959, followed by the disbandment of the Territorial Battalion in 1969 and its Cadre in 1975.

The book serves various purposes. It will be of great interest to surviving members of the original Regiment and those who have served in, or who are serving with, its successor, The King's Own Royal Border Regiment. It will capture the imagination of readers of all ages, whether they have a military background or not, and it will be invaluable to military researchers world-wide due to the wealth of photographic data that it contains. The historical asset is due to the wide coverage that it gives to personalities, uniforms, weapons and the way of life in peace and war, and also to the description of individual acts of valour that earned the major gallantry awards. To this information are added the 100 Battle Honours that were earned by the Regiment during its 279 years of existence.

At a time when the value of the Regimental system is under public debate, this work well illustrates its worth by the wide coverage of Regular, Militia, Territorial, Cadet and Allied Regiment activity. Stuart is to be congratulated for his idea of creating this work, and for his perseverance in completing it after painstaking research, his dedication to the Regiment and his professional competence as a writer.

INTRODUCTION AND ACKNOWLEDGEMENTS

It is probably true to say that most families in the United Kingdom have had some contact with the British Army, and many have a passing interest in it. The aim of this book is to provide an insight into the history and traditions of one of the oldest Regiments in the British Army, The King's Own Royal Regiment (Lancaster). It traces the history of the Regiment from its formation in 1680, through the amalgamation of the Regular Battalion with the Border Regiment in 1959 to form The King's Own Royal Border Regiment, to the survival of the Territorial Battalion until 1969 and its Cadre until 1975.

The choice of photographs is very much a personal one, and without doubt the hardest decision has been what to leave out. The choice has been governed by the quality of the original image, the variety of subject and the condition of the photograph. Unfortunately, for some periods, particularly during the First and Second World Wars, photographs of particular battalions or locations are unavailable. Moreover, since the book is principally pictorial, it should not be seen as a definitive history, but rather as complementary to the three-volume work written by the Cowper family.

Having worked with the Regimental Museum collections over the last five years, I have become familiar both with the Regiment's history and also with the lives and service of many of the individuals who have served in it. To this end I have endeavoured to detail not only the events and traditions of the Regiment, but also, where possible, to name individuals in the photographs, rather than just provide anonymous captions. I hope therefore that this book will be seen as the history of one Regimental Family, and is dedicated to those who served in it, and, in the time-honoured tradition of regimental pride and loyalty, believed The King's Own to be second to none. I hope also that it will be of interest to those who have served in the Regiment and their families, to those with a general interest in military history, and to people from Lancashire and the North West, from whence the Regiment traditionally drew its recruits.

The establishment of the Museum of The King's Own Royal Regiment (Lancaster) in Lancaster City Museum in 1929 provided the foundation of the Regimental Archives, from which many of the photographs in this book have been selected. Over the last 60 years the photographic and documentary holdings in the archives have grown tremendously. Much of this is due to the energies of former officers on the Regimental Museum and Historical Committees, in particular Colonels L. I. Cowper OBE, C. W. Grover, G. T. E. Keith DSO OBE, and R. P. F. White MC, the efforts of former Curators, G. F. Bland FRGS FLA (1929–1955), Mrs E. Tyson FMA (1965–1983), and W. G. Watson MA (1983–1986), and the generosity of many former members of the Regiment and their families.

Many people have contributed towards the production of this book with the loan or donation of photographs, the identification of individuals, locations and dates, and by providing information, help and encouragement, without which the book would not have appeared. I am particularly grateful to the following, many of whom served in The King's Own and its successor The King's Own Royal Border Regiment:

Brigadier A. J. Addy, Misses C. and S. Armstrong, Cliff Blood, C. Bonnell, E. Bostock, Captain F. Boulter, Captain G. Brady, Alec Campbell, Jane Carmichael MA (Imperial War Museum), Major R. Cockroft MC, Captain S. Cole, Colonel J. G. de Cordova OBE, Brigadier D. H. Davies MC, Lieutenant-Colonel P. E. Dew, Captain H. F. Duckworth, Brigadier D. E. Dunand, George Ellwood BEM, Major R. J. T. Evans, O. Frear, Major C. H. W. Gray, Captain J. Hands, Lieutenant-Colonel J. M. Hardy, Major D. Harrison, Major J. F. Hart, Joe Heath, Vic Holmes, Bob Howson, Ernie Huddart, Tom Hunt, Lieutenant-Colonel J. A. Hunton-Carter OBE, Graham Jackson, A. Jones, Captain H. M. R. Jones, John Lawrence, Colonel D. B. Long MC KStJ TD DL, Frank Marley, Tom Marsland, Lieutenant-Colonel D. J. Martin, Colonel R. K. May FMA (Curator of The Border Regiment–King's Own Royal Border Regiment Museum), Danny Miller, Laurie Milner (Imperial War Museum), Major S. Murphy, Bill Owen, Alan Pawson, Ted Procter, Jimmy Quirk, Dick Radcliffe, Major P. V. Roberts, the late Colonel W. V. H. Robins DSO, Fred Robinson, Lieutenant-Colonel W. A. Robinson OBE, Ronnie Rogerson, Captain C. L. Rostron, Lieutenant-Colonel H. H. K. Rowe DSO, Lieutenant-Colonel A. F. Royle TD, Colonel V. F. Royle ERD DL, Alan Sandham (Lancaster and Morecambe Newspapers), George Simmons, F. Snape, Peter Stanley (Australian War Memorial, Canberra), Vic Stewart, Lieutenant-Colonel C. C. Stock, Peter Taylor, Captain P. Taylor MBE, the late Lieutenant-Colonel W. T. P. Tilly, Major T. C. V. Todd MBE TD, Major D. Warren MC, Malcolm White, Eric Wilkinson, Happy Wilkinson, Captain C. W. Wingrove, Alan Woodward.

The author also wishes to acknowledge the help given by the staffs of, and the permission to use photographs from, the Australian War Memorial, Canberra, the Commonwealth War Graves Commission, the Department of Photographs at the Imperial War Museum, Lancaster and Morecambe Newspapers, the National Gallery of Victoria, Melbourne, and the National Maritime Museum. I am grateful to Brigadier James Howard CBE, Regimental Secretary, and Captain Ian Banks, Assistant Regimental Secretary, of The King's Own Royal Border Regiment at Carlisle for their help during the project. My thanks are also due to Major-General N. St G. Gribbon OBE, who kindly wrote the Foreword and read and made several useful comments on the draft. Lieutenant-Colonel T. Jarvis-Bicknell MBE, the Commanding Officer of the 1st Battalion The King's Own Royal Border Regiment, kindly gave permission to use The Forlorn Hope on the front cover.

I am grateful to my colleagues at Lancaster City Museums, Sue Ashworth, Malcolm Davies, Paul Thompson and Andrew White, for their help and encouragement, and Helen Griffiths and Sandra Wilkinson for typing and revising the many drafts of the manuscript. Thanks are due to Norwyn Photographic of Preston for copying a large number of original illustrations and photographs. Silver Link Publishing Ltd of Great Addington in Northamptonshire, particularly their editor Will Adams, receive my thanks for their help and patience in producing the book. To Norman Rowlinson, who has worked at the Museum as a volunteer for the last two years, I owe a special debt of gratitude. He has spent many hours sorting through the photographic collections, researching and checking numerous items of information, reading the drafts and providing much help and encouragement. Finally my family deserve a thank-you for putting up with 'Daddy and the book' during many evenings and weekends over the last year.

All the photographs, except where stated, are from the Regimental Museum Archives. Copies of these and other photographs in the archives are available on application to the Museum. Copies of photographs from the Imperial War Museum, indicated by 'IWM' and a negative number, are available by application to the Department of Photographs, Imperial War Museum, Lambeth Road, London SE1 6HZ.

The royalties from the sale of the book will go to the Regimental Museum.

Chapter 1

1680-1850

TANGIEREENES, BARRELLS AND LIONS

The history of The King's Own begins in 1680, when Charles (Fitzcharles), Earl of Plymouth, a natural son of King Charles II, was appointed Colonel of a new Regiment of Foot raised for the defence of Tangier, which at that time was besieged by the Moroccan Emperor. The Crown had acquired the Colony as part of the dowry of Catherine de Braganza on her marriage to Charles II. The officers commanding the 16 companies of the new Regiment were issued with a copy of the Royal Warrant of 13 July (old style) which authorised each of them '. . . by beat of Drum to raise three score volunteers to serve as private soldiers in your company of the Regiment now to be raised for our Services att Tangier of which our Dearley beloved naturelle sonne Charles Earle of Plymouth is Collonell . . .'

Ten companies of the Regiment were raised mainly in the London area and concentrated at Clerkenwell under Lieutenant-Colonel Piercy Kirke, while six companies raised in the West Country met at Plymouth under Major Charles Trelawny. Thirteen officers and many of the men had previously served with Monmouth's Royal English Regiment in the Netherlands. The Regiment arrived in Tangier on 28 December 1680 to find a truce in operation. Their Colonel, who had been serving in Tangier as a volunteer, had died in November; and Colonelcy passed to Kirke, and

Charles Trelawny was appointed Lieutenant-Colonel. In 1681, Kirke assisted the Governor in negotiating a Peace Treaty and in 1682 became Governor. He also assumed the Colonelcy of the Old or First Tangier Regiment, later the Queen's Royal Regiment (West Surrey). Subsequently Trelawny succeeded him as Colonel of the New or Second Tangier Regiment (it was common practice for Regiments to be referred to by their Colonel's name until 1751).

The garrison suffered from losses through sickness and death, a lack of provisions and recruits, and substantial arrears of pay. In 1683 Parliament refused to sanction further expenditure for the garrison and Lord Dartmouth arrived in October to supervise the dismantling of the defences and the evacuation. Trelawny's Regiment participated in a review of all the available troops and sailors from the Fleet to conceal the withdrawal from the Moors and provide a show of force. The Grenadier Company of the Regiment was amongst the rear-guard, which embarked for England in February 1684. On its arrival in April, Trelawny's Regiment was transferred to the English establishment, reduced to 12 companies and retitled 'The Duchess of York and Albany's Regiment'.

In February 1685 Charles II died and was succeeded by his brother James, Duke of York, as

King James II. Fears in Parliament, the Army and the country about the King's Catholicism were overshadowed by the landing of James, Duke of Monmouth, at Lyme Regis on 21 June; an illegitimate son of Charles II, he claimed the throne, but despite a few minor successes was unable to defeat the main Royal Army or win substantial support. Five companies of Trelawny's, now the Queen's Regiment of Foot, formed part of the Royal Army under John Churchill and Lord Feversham, which routed Monmouth's Army at the Battle of Sedgemoor near Bridgwater in Somerset, on 16 July.

James II, however, gradually lost support by filling both government and military positions with his favourites, who were predominantly Catholic. His interference in a court martial involving the desertion of a soldier of Trelawny's, who was subsequently executed, caused great discontent in the Regiment. The birth of a Prince of Wales in June 1688 and the arrest and imprisonment of seven Bishops in the Tower of London for refusing to read the proclamation for the Liberty of Conscience, provoked even greater opposition; one of the Bishops, Jonathan Trelawny, was the brother of the Regiment's Colonel. Popular feeling in the West Country was so strong that a song, 'And Shall Trelawny Die', was written; the Bishops were later acquitted. The tune of the song was subsequently adopted as the Slow March of The King's Own (see Appendix 6).

Charles Trelawny was one of several officers in the Army who solicited the Protestant Prince William of Orange and Princess Mary (daughter of Charles II) to land in England. William landed at Torbay on 5 November 1688 and by the end of the month most of the officers of Trelawny's had transferred their allegiance to him. At the beginning of January 1689 James II fled to France, and William succeeded him as King William III. It is a Regimental tradition that the new king granted the Regiment its badge, the Lion of England, for being one of the first to go over to him. The Regiment subsequently served with William's Army against James and his French allies in Ireland, at the Battle of the Boyne near Dundalk on 11 July 1690, and the sieges of Cork and Kinsale in 1690 and Limerick in 1691.

In 1692 the Regiment joined William's forces in Flanders against the French King Louis XIV, who still supported James's claim to the English throne. It was present at the Battles of Steenkirk (1692), Landen (1693) and at the siege of the town and citadel of Namur, where the Grenadier Company distinguished itself. NAMUR 1695 became the Regiment's earliest Battle Honour although it was not granted until 1910.

Trelawny's returned home in 1696, but war against Louis XIV broke out again in 1702 over the succession to the Spanish throne. The Regiment was present at the capture of Cadiz and the attack on French and Spanish shipping at Vigo. In 1703 it was placed on the Marine establishment, and took part in the capture of Gibraltar and the defence of the colony from October 1704 to May 1705; GIBRALTAR 1704-5 became the Regiment's second Battle Honour, granted in 1909. Later the Regiment or detachments were present and took part in several operations on the east coast of Spain — the captures of Barcelona (1705), Carthagena (1705), Alicante (1706), Iveca and Majorca (1706), Lerida (1707), and Sardinia and Minorca (1708). In 1710 the Regiment returned to the Army establishment as The Queen's Own Regiment.

At the end of August 1711, having been ordered to Canada, the expedition was wrecked during a gale in the St Lawrence River and over 200 of the Regiment and members of their families perished.

Apart from two brief periods of service in the Netherlands, the Regiment remained at home until 1753. In July 1715 King George I conferred upon the Regiment its new title 'The King's Own'. In September the First Jacobite Rebellion broke out in support of the claim to the throne by James Stuart, James II's son, who landed in Scotland in December. Although the Regiment was not involved, the Lancashire Militia, first raised in 1689, supported the Royal Army in the defeat of the Rebel Army at the Battle of Preston on 12 November. The Militia, which suffered over 100 casualties, later became part of The King's Own in 1881.

Thirty years later, in July 1745, James Stuart's son, Charles Edward Stuart (Bonnie Prince Charlie), landed in Scotland to claim the throne for his father. The Regiment, now known as Barrell's after its Colonel, General William Barrell, joined General Wade's forces in pursuit of the Prince's Army, which, having defeated a Royal Army at Prestonpans on 2 October and having advanced as far as Derby, was now retreating north. The

Lancashire Militia, embodied during the Rebellion, assisted the Duke of Cumberland's Army and was present at the Battle of Clifton Moor near Penrith on 18 December. At the Battle of Falkirk on 17 January 1746, Barrell's, supported by four other Regiments, stood firm against a furious charge by the Highlanders who, having already beaten off the Royal Army's cavalry, threatened to rout the Army.

On 16 April, at the decisive Battle of Culloden, Barrell's, with Munro's on its right, bore the brunt of the Highland charge, supported by Wolfe's on its left flank and Bligh's and Sempill's to the rear and right. An extract from a contemporary publication, *Particulars of the Battle of Culloden,* records that 'General Barrell's regiment gained the greatest reputation imaginable at the late engagement, the best of the Clans having made their strongest efforts to break them without effect; for the old "Tangiereenes" bravely repulsed those boasters with a dreadful slaughter and convinced them that their broadswords and targets are unequalled to the musket and bayonet when in the hands of veterans who are determined to use them.'

The Regiment remained in Scotland until September 1751, and in the Royal Warrant regulating the clothing of the Army issued in July of that year, it was styled 'The 4th or King's Own Regiment'. It was fourth in the order of seniority of the Line Infantry Regiments and had received the alternative title, 4th Foot, in a Royal Warrant of September 1743.

Posted to the Island of Minorca on garrison duty in 1753, the Regiment served under the octogenarian General Blackeney in the defence of Fort St Philip from April until the end of July 1756. In recognition of the defenders' bravery, the French commander allowed them to march out with all the honours of war, following their surrender. A 2nd Battalion of the Regiment was raised in 1756, which in 1758 became the 62nd Foot (Wiltshire Regiment). That year The King's Own sailed for the West Indies, where it remained for the next five years. It took part in the capture of the French and Spanish-held islands of Guadeloupe (1759), Dominique (1761), Martinique and Havanna (1762). GUADELOUPE 1759 was the Regiment's third Battle Honour, granted in 1909.

In 1764 The King's Own returned to England, where it remained until 1774, when it sailed for Boston in North America. It was present at the first actions of the American War of Independence at Lexington and Concord in April 1775 then, on 17 June, the Grenadier and Light Companies fought at the Battle of Bunker Hill on the Charleston Heights above Boston. The King's Own remained in Boston until its evacuation in March 1776, when it sailed for Halifax, proceeding from there to New York with General Howe's forces. In July 1777 the Regiment sailed with Howe's forces via the Chesapeake River to attack Washington's Army in Delaware and Pennsylvania. It was present at the victories of Germantown on 11 September and Brandywine on 4 October, which allowed the British to occupy Philadelphia. Following France's entry into the war and the threat to British possessions, the Regiment formed part of an expedition to the West Indies, where it participated in the landing on and capture of St Lucia from the French; ST LUCIA 1778 was granted as the Regiment's fourth Battle Honour in 1909.

The Regiment came home in 1780 and spent seven years in Ireland before returning to North America for ten years' garrison duty in Newfoundland, Nova Scotia and Quebec. On the return journey to England, the ship carrying Battalion Headquarters was captured by a French privateer. To prevent the Colours from being captured, Mrs Surgeon Maguire weighted them with her flat-irons and threw them overboard.

In 1799 the Regiment was expanded to three Battalions and John Pitt, 2nd Earl of Chatham, became its Colonel, a position he held until 1835. The three Battalions served in one Brigade, commanded by Lord Chatham, as part of an allied expedition to the Netherlands against the French in the autumn of 1799, which included the Battle of Egmont-on-Zee on 2 October. Both the 2nd and 3rd Battalions were disbanded in 1802, only for the 2nd Battalion to be re-raised in 1804 following the resumption of the war with Napoleon.

The Lancashire Militia was embodied for home defence between 1759 and 1762, 1778 and 1783 and from 1793 throughout the Revolutionary and Napoleonic Wars until 1816. During these periods it was stationed at many places throughout the country and had been granted the title 'Royal' in 1761. In 1799 it was expanded to three Regiments, the 1st Regiment having its headquarters in Lancaster. A number of officers and men enlisted for the Regular Army from the Militia. In addition, during the Napoleonic Wars a number of local Volunteer units were formed for home defence: The Loyal Lancaster Volunteers (1797-1808), the Ulverston Volunteer Infantry (1803-1806), and The Lonsdale Regiment of Local Militia (1808-1816).

The 1st Battalion participated in several expeditions, to Hanover in 1805, Copenhagen in 1807 and Gothenberg in 1808. Following Napoleon's invasion of Spain and Portugal to enforce the Continental System, which forbade European ships to enter British ports and vice versa, an expedition of 11,000 men, including the 1st Battalion King's Own, was sent to Spain in July 1808. Commanded by Sir John Moore, it advanced towards Madrid, but was forced by an enormous French Army to retreat north-west to Corunna on the coast. Averaging 17 miles a day and losing men from cold and exposure, Moore's troops reached Corunna on 11 January; The King's Own only lost 14 men during the retreat.

With the arrival of the Fleet to evacuate the troops on 14 January, the French under Marshal Soult decided to attack on the 16th. The King's Own were on the right flank in Bentinck's Brigade, and at one point, to prevent encirclement by the French, moved the four companies of the right wing back to form a defensive flank. Moore commented to the commanding officer, Lieutenant-Colonel James Wynch, 'That is exactly what I wanted to be done. I am glad to see a Regiment there in which I can place so much confidence'. The French were held off and the troops evacuated, but Moore had been fatally wounded. CORUNNA was the first Battle Honour to be granted to the Regiment in 1812.

In July 1810 both Battalions of the Regiment formed part of the Walcheren expedition to occupy the islands in the Scheldt Estuary and destroy French defences, dock and ship-building facilities in Flushing. A widespread epidemic of fever, together with disagreements between the commanders and the reinforcing of the French Army, caused the expedition to be abandoned in September. After recuperating, the 1st Battalion joined Wellington's forces in the Peninsula in November 1810, while the 2nd Battalion went to North Africa. Apart from minor actions the 1st Battalion was not heavily engaged until the spring of 1812, when it joined the forces besieging the fortress of Badajoz, 100 miles east of Lisbon on the River Guadiana.

On 6 April The King's Own were ordered to take part in the assault on the Bastion of San Vicente, one of eight in the perimeter defences. Major Piper led the Battalion in scaling the walls; on finding that the ladders were too short, the men at the top were pushed up on the shoulders of those below and over the ramparts. After severe hand-to-hand fighting the fortress fell; The King's Own suffered 44 officers and other ranks killed and 188 wounded. Later in the year both Battalions were present at the Battle of Salamanca on 22 July, where their discipline was noted as they marched over a quarter of a mile under heavy fire 'with a degree of silence, regularity and precision never surpassed in any of its field days in England'. Following the failure to capture Burgos, the Army withdrew and morale at the end of 1812 was very low. However, in the spring Wellington's forces advanced north and defeated the French at the Battle of Vittoria on 21 June 1813. The 1st Battalion King's Own, in Robinson's Brigade, took part in the attack on the village of Gamara Mayor.

By July they had reached San Sebastian, one of two fortresses which had to be captured before Wellington's Army could cross the Pyrenees into France. After several unsuccessful assaults The King's Own and the remainder of Robinson's Brigade, led by the Forlorn Hope commanded by Lieutenant Francis Maguire of the King's Own, stormed the breach on 31 August, and on 9 September the remaining members of the garrison surrendered. The 1st Battalion took part in the battles of the campaign, named after the rivers that were crossed, during the advance over the Pyrenees into France — the Bidaossa on 7 October, Nivelle on 10 November and Nive on 9-13 December 1813. It formed part of the army which blockaded the French town of Bayonne whilst the final battles of the campaign were fought. In April Napoleon abdicated, and on 15 May The King's Own marched into Bayonne.

However, in May the 1st Battalion embarked at Bordeaux to fight in the United States, which had declared war on Britain in 1811 because of the boarding and searching of American ships by the British Navy. Arriving in Chesapeake Bay, The King's Own fought at the Battle of Bladensburg on 23 August 1814, which led to the capture of Washington. An advance towards Baltimore was abandoned and the Army embarked for Jamaica. On 8 January 1815 the Regiment took part in the attack on New Orleans and suffered its worst casualties in a battle up to that date, with 23 officers and 300 other ranks killed or wounded; the attack was abandoned. After other minor engagements the 1st Battalion returned to England, arriving at Deal on 18 May 1815.

The Battalion was re-equipped, re-clothed and made up to strength from the 2nd Battalion, then on 12 June it landed at Ostend and was ordered to join Wellington's Army against Napoleon. Napoleon had escaped from exile in Elba, re-established himself as Emperor and reformed his army. The King's Own marched to Ghent, where they joined Lambert's 10th Brigade, and on to Brussels. The Battalion arrived at Waterloo on the morning of 18 June with 'band playing and Colours flying', having marched 48 miles in 30 hours, and was the only Battalion which had recently served in America to fight at Waterloo. It was in reserve until 3 pm when it was brought into the line opposite the gravel pit, near the farm of La Haye Sainte. After heavy fighting and the repulse of the attack by the French Imperial Guard, the Regiment took part in the general advance in the evening, and, with the rest of the Brigade, cleared the gravel pit and the farm. Out of a strength of 669 officers and men, the Regiment suffered 134 casualties. Thus one of the longest and most arduous periods of active service in the Regiment's history ended.

The King's own added BADAJOZ, SALAMANCA, VITTORIA, ST SEBASTIAN, NIVE, PENINSULA, BLADENSBURG and WATERLOO to its other Battle Honours. In addition, each officer and man who had fought in the Waterloo Campaign received a silver medal and was allowed two years' service for an increase of pay or for a pension when discharged. However, the survivors of the Peninsula battles had to wait until 1848 before they received any recognition with the award of the Military General Service Medal, but 321 former officers and men of the Regiment lived to receive it.

The 1st Battalion marched to Paris after Waterloo and remained with the Army of Occupation in France until October 1818. The 2nd Battalion, which had been in England since February 1813, was disbanded in December 1815. From 1815 until it embarked for the Crimea, The King's Own saw very little active service but a great deal of garrison duty to defend Britain's growing Empire. It went to the West Indies for garrison duties from 1819 to 1826, during which time nearly 200 officers and men died of yellow fever. This was followed by a brief but uneventful period of active service in Portugal from December 1826 until April 1828, and home service until 1831. In 1831 and 1832 the Regiment went out by detachments to Australia as guards on convict ships and to provide garrisons for the settlements in New South Wales and Tasmania. The Regiment went to India in 1837, returning to England in 1848.

A grenadier of the Earl of Plymouth's Regiment, *circa* 1684, from a watercolour based on a reconstruction by Clifford Walton.

Troops demolishing the mole and harbour installations at Tangier, prior to the evacuation of the fort and defences in 1684, from an oil painting by Dirck Stoop. *Reproduced by kind permission of the National Maritime Museum.*

Charles Trelawny, who joined the Regiment as a Major on its formation in July 1680, having previously served in Monmouth's Royal English Regiment in the 1670s. In November 1680 he succeeded Piercy Kirke as Lieutenant-Colonel of the Regiment and was appointed Colonel in April 1682. He held this position until 1692, apart from a short period in December 1688 following the landing of William of Orange, when he was replaced by Sir Charles Orby on the orders of King James II. His brother Henry Trelawny, who also joined the Regiment on its formation and commanded it, was Colonel from 1692 to 1702.

The landing of William of Orange at Torbay on 5 November 1688.

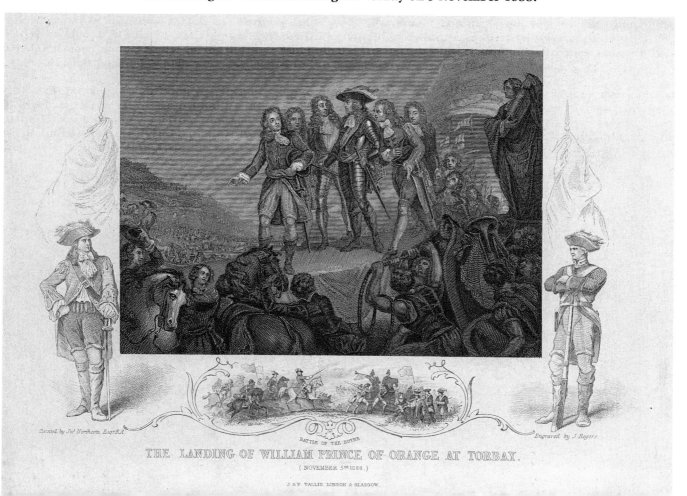

Painted by Jas Northcote, Esqr RA.

BATTLE OF THE BOYNE

Engraved by J Rogers

THE LANDING OF WILLIAM PRINCE OF ORANGE AT TORBAY.

(NOVEMBER 5TH 1688.)

J & F. TALLIS, LONDON & GLASGOW.

The Battle of Vigo Bay, October 1702, from an oil painting by Ludolf Bakhuizen. The Regiment took part in this joint naval and military operation to destroy French and Spanish shipping in this harbour on the north-west coast of Spain. The Regiment received prize money of £589 3s 6d as its share of the booty taken there. *Reproduced by kind permission of the National Maritime Museum.*

The *Royal Katherine,* from an oil painting attributed to Isaac Sailmaker. The Regiment served on this ship as Marines in 1704. *Reproduced by kind permission of the National Maritime Museum.*

Private man of a Battalion company of The King's Own Regiment, 1742, from a watercolour by F. W. Barry after an original in the Royal Collections.

The Battle of Culloden, 16 April 1746, from a watercolour copy after the original painting 'An Incident in the Rebellion of 1745' by David Morier in the Royal Collections. The painting depicts the grenadiers of Barrell's Regiment receiving the Highland charge, which initially broke their ranks. The platoons of the Regiment either stood their ground or fell back to reform on Sempill's Regiment behind them. The fighting was extremely savage and the Regiment suffered a third of the Royal Army's casualties, with 18 killed and 108 wounded. For 40 years thereafter, the seal of the Regiment bore the word CULLODEN engraved below the Lion of England, in recognition of the Regiment's gallant conduct during the battle.

Grenadier, 4th or King's Own Regiment, dressed according to the Royal Warrant of 1751. From a watercolour by F. W. Barry, *circa* 1933, after an original by David Morier in the Royal Collections.

A contemporary satirical print reflecting the strict discipline imposed by Lieutenant-Colonel Robert Rich on his Regiment after Culloden. It must have been some time before Rich recovered from his wounds and rejoined his Regiment, but the print probably dates from *circa* 1749 or earlier, since the Regiment is referred to by the name of its Colonel, William Barrell. Lieutenant-Colonel Rich gave up command when he assumed the Colonelcy of the Regiment on Barrell's death in August 1749. The soldiers who are drawn up to witness the punishment wear barrels, an allusion to the Regiment's name. The castle in the background suggests Edinburgh as the location, although the Regiment was based in several places during its stay in Scotland from April 1746 to September 1751. The soldier on the left laments, 'I'v not been whipt since ye coll. left us'. The prisoner tied to the tripod of halberds says, 'I wish I'd been kill'd by the Rebels', whilst the drummer intercedes, 'Coll. he behaved well at Culloden'.

Sir Robert Rich (1714–1785), Colonel of the Regiment 1749–1756, from an oil painting by Arthur Devis, *circa* 1756. He was badly wounded whilst commanding Barrell's Regiment at Culloden, losing his left hand and almost his right arm. Rich bequeathed the portrait to his chaplain, John Duncan, who carried him from the battlefield. A descendant, Miss Duncan, gave the painting to Sir Robert Rich 4th Bt, and Lady Rich presented it to the Regimental Museum in 1937.

Milestone erected by the Regiment at Malagan, near Glenshiel; it was later moved to Aultachruin. The King's Own were stationed in Scotland from April 1767 until March 1773 and were employed on road-building at Glenshiel during the summer of 1771.

Medal of the Loyal and Friendly Society of the Blew and Orange. This Society was formed *circa* 1733 by officers of the Regiment as an expression of loyalty to the House of Hanover and in memory of King William III. During its existence the Prince of Wales (later George IV), Prince William Henry (later William IV), and the Duke of York became members of the Society, its membership being open to those outside the Regiment. The Society dined four times a year and each member wore his medal fastened to a button of his waistcoat by two narrow ribbons, one of blue, the other of orange. These became the colours of the Regiment, blue representing the Royal connection and orange the link with William III. The last recorded dinner of the Society was in 1801.

Mrs Elizabeth Maguire (1775–1857) features prominently in the Regiment's history. Her husband Francis, who died in Java in 1811, was surgeon to the 4th Foot from 1789 to 1806, whilst her son Francis was killed leading the Forlorn Hope at St Sebastian in 1813. A second son, Peter, died at sea. In September 1797 she was on board the transport *The Three Sisters* bringing the Headquarters of the Regiment home from Canada, when it was chased and captured by a French privateer. To prevent the Colours from falling into enemy hands, Mrs Maguire wrapped them around her flat-irons and dropped them into the sea. She was imprisoned at Brest with her husband and two sons, Francis and Peter, and others of the Regiment until her release in September 1798. Her first daughter was born during captivity.

FOURTH REGIMENT of FOOT.

GENERAL MORRISON, *Colonel of the* FOURTH (or the KINGS own) REGIMENT of FOOT, *and to the* OTHER OFFICERS *of that Regiment. This representation of their Uniform is most respectfully dedicated.* *By their obedient Servants.* THE PROPRIETORS. London, September, 1799.

Officer, 4th Foot, 1799, from a print by J. Carpenter.

Other ranks shako-plate, 4th Foot, 1800–12, found during deepening operations in a well at Niza, Portugal, in 1899.

A Colour of the Hesse-Darmstadt Regiment in the French Service taken by Private George Hatton, Light Company 4th Foot, during the capture of the St Vicente bastion at the siege of Badajoz on 6 April 1812. Two Colours of this Regiment were presented to the Duke of Wellington, who gave Hatton a £20 reward and desired that he be promoted. Hatton's comrades presented him with a silver medal (right). The second Colour was captured by Private John Kelton, who also received a silver regimental medal from his comrades. These Colours hung in the Royal Hospital at Chelsea until 1947, when they were restored to the Regiment and placed in the Regimental Museum. From a watercolour by Miss S. B. Steel, 1936.

'Vittoria, 21 June 1813: Village of Gamara Mayor, carried by the 4th, 47th and 59th Regiments of Robinson's Brigade'. This is the original pencil and charcoal sketch by J. P. Beadle RA for his oil painting, which was exhibited at the Royal Academy in 1913. The French held the village and the bridge beyond, one of two which had to be taken to close a possible line of retreat for the enemy. Robinson's Brigade on the left of the attack comprised three Battalions, the 1/4th, 2/59th and 2/47th Regiments (all closely associated with Lancashire after 1881 as the 1st Battalion King's Own Royal Lancaster, 2nd Battalion East Lancashire and 1st Battalion Loyal North Lancashire Regiments). Led by Lieutenant-Colonel Brooke, the 4th and the other Regiments took the village at the point of the bayonet, although the bridge remained in enemy hands despite three heroic assaults. The French were eventually forced to retreat by Wellington's columns in the centre and on the right.

The picture depicts, on the left, men and an officer of the 47th on foot, led by Captain Livesey of the 47th on horseback. In the centre Lieutenant-Colonel Brooke, also on horseback, leads men of the 4th through the middle of the village. Near him is the Ensign with the 4th's Regimental Colour. A Colour Sergeant bends down to retrieve the 4th's King's Colour from the fallen Ensign. On the right, men of the 4th fight with French troops on the other side of the wall. The artist gave the sketch to Lieutenant-Colonel A. D. Thorne, whose great-uncle, Lieutenant George Thorne, was killed at Gamara Mayor, one of the Regiment's 91 casualties.

'The Forlorn Hope' — the artist's pencil sketch for the oil painting illustrated on the front cover. The painting was commissioned by past and present officers of The King's Own for 100 guineas and exhibited by the artist, Mr J. P. Beadle RA, at the Royal Academy in 1912. Originally titled 'St Sebastian, August 1913', the painting depicts the Forlorn Hope of Robinson's Brigade led by Lieutenant Francis Maguire and men of the 4th Foot, at the moment of his death at the foot of the great breach on 31 August. The Forlorn Hope was followed by the Light Companies and the remainder of the Brigade in two columns. The initial assault failed with heavy casualties, but was resumed successfully after a heavy artillery bombardment. The Regiment suffered severe casualties with five officers and 117 men killed, and six officers and 170 men wounded. Major-General Robinson wrote: 'The Fourth led and perhaps in the whole history of the war there cannot be found a stronger instance of courage and obedience to orders'.

Francis Maguire's death was widely mourned. He was appointed as an Ensign in the Regiment in 1804 aged 12 and joined it aged 16 in the Peninsula, where he served with distinction and was mentioned for bravery at Albuhera, Vittoria and Salamanca. Maguire, who had previously volunteered twice to lead a Forlorn Hope, was killed on his 21st birthday. The artist's sketch shows Maguire wearing a shako, whilst the painting correctly shows him wearing a cocked hat. The sketch was given by the artist to Lieutenant-Colonel A. D. Thorne, whose widow presented it to the Regimental Museum. The original painting hangs in the Officers' Mess of the 1st Battalion King's Own Royal Border Regiment.

The medals of Lieutenant-Colonel Thomas Piper CB, 1783–1822. Piper fought throughout the Peninsula campaign, was wounded at St Sebastian and on the Nive, and died of yellow fever whilst commanding the 1st Battalion in the West Indies. The medals are the Order of the Bath Companion's Badge, the Field Officer's Gold Medal for Salamanca, with bars for St Sebastian and the Nive, and a Peninsula Gold Cross, one of two awarded to the Regiment, for Salamanca, Badajoz, St Sebastian and Nive.

The memorial at St Sebastian, *circa* 1930. The only one to British troops who died in Spain, it is located on the slopes of Monte Orgullo (Urgull) and was unveiled by the Spanish Queen on 28 September 1924. The figure with arm raised, leading the group representing a Forlorn Hope, is Lieutenant Francis Maguire. Beneath the group is the inscription in English and Spanish: 'England has confided to us her Glorious Dead, Our Gratitude will Guard Their Eternal Repose.' Behind the sculpture is a tablet with the arms of Great Britain and Spain and the inscription: 'In memory of the gallant British Soldiers who gave their lives for the greatness of their own country and for the independence of Spain.'

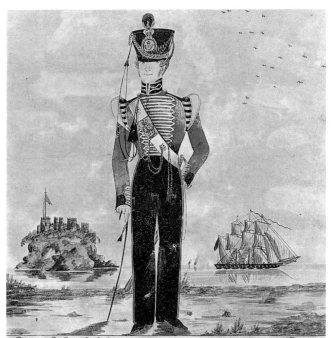

A portrait of Henry Watts, of the Light Company 4th Foot, painted in March or April 1831 before his departure for Australia. The inscription reads: 'Henry Watts, 4th King's Own, Lions of England, Dear Parents when you see this remember me And bear me in your mind When i am far in a Foreign Clime.' On the reverse of the picture is written: 'Painted by Charles Dean late 15th Regiment . . . for H Watts . . . Chatham, Kent.' Between March 1831 and July 1832 the Regiment sailed to New South Wales in detachments as guards on board convict ships, and a number of officers and men chose to settle in Australia when the Regiment left for India in 1837. Amongst these was Captain William Lonsdale, who in 1835 had been sent as Police Magistrate by the Governor of New South Wales to the settlement of Port Philip. The settlement later developed into the City of Melbourne, where the main street bears Lonsdale's name and the entrance to the harbour is known as Lonsdale Point.

Chapter 2

1850-1880

FROM THE CRIMEA TO THE CAPE

In March 1854 The King's Own were placed in readiness for service overseas due to the growing tension between Russia and Turkey. On the 8th the Regiment embarked for Malta, arriving just before war was declared, and proceeded thence, via Gallipoli and Varna, to the Crimean Peninsula on the northern shore of the Black Sea. It arrived there in September and formed part of the British 3rd Division. The objective was the Russian fortress of Sebastopol.

The King's Own were present at the Battle of the Alma on 20 September, when they supported the Guards Brigade. The victory cleared the Russian positions dominating the valley of the River Alma, and the Regiment settled down to siege warfare until the fall of Sebastopol in September 1855. The Regiment was also present at the Battle of Inkerman on 5 November, when the Russians launched a surprise attack on the British trenches, although it was mainly in reserve. The campaign is chiefly remembered for the appalling conditions under which the troops lived and fought. The terrible winter of 1854-5, combined with the lack of accommodation, clothing, provisions and medical care, caused far more casualties than the fighting during the war: 39 officers and men of the Regiment were killed or died of wounds, 306 died of disease and 278 were invalided home.

Private Thomas Grady won the Regiment's first

Victoria Cross (see page 178), and 16 NCOs and men received the medal for Distinguished Conduct in the Field (DCM). Other decorations awarded to officers and other ranks included two CBs, five Legion D'Honneur, five Sardinian War Medals and nine French War Medals. All ranks received the British Crimea Medal with one or more of the clasps Alma, Inkerman, Balaklava and Sebastopol, and the Turkish Crimea Medal. The Regiment received the Battle Honours ALMA, INKERMAN and SEVASTOPOL. The 1st Regiment of Royal Lancashire Militia, which had been re-activated in 1852, volunteered for overseas service during the war and carried out garrison duty on Corfu, Cephalonia and Zante (the Ionian Islands) in 1855–6; over 280 men died from cholera on Corfu. For its services, the Regiment was awarded the Honour MEDITERRANEAN on its Colours.

The King's Own reformed at Aldershot in August 1856 and the following year the 1st Battalion left for Mauritius. Following the outbreak of the Indian Mutiny in May 1857, the right wing of the Battalion embarked for Bombay in September, but saw little action apart from the unsuccessful attempt to capture Fort Beyt, on the island of Beyt, south-east of Karachi, on 2 April 1858. Seven officers and 202 other ranks received the Indian Mutiny Medal without clasp. In January 1859 the left wing of the Battalion joined the right wing in Ahmedabad for a further nine years' service in India.

On 23 October 1857 the Regiment formed a 2nd Battalion which remained in England until fully recruited in 1859, when it sailed for foreign service in the Ionian Islands, Malta and Nova Scotia before returning to England in May 1869. In 1859 and 1860, companies of the Lancashire Rifle Volunteers were formed as part of the widespread revival of auxiliary forces throughout the country. In north Lancashire companies were raised in Lancaster, Ulverston, Barrow-in-Furness, Dalton, Cartmel and Rossall, which by 1863 had been consolidated as the 5th (Administrative) Battalion Lancashire Rifle Volunteers. The unit would become part of The King's Own in 1883.

In September 1867 the 1st Battalion was ordered to prepare for active service in Abyssinia (Ethiopia). The Abyssinian Emperor, Theodore, had imprisoned a number of British subjects, including two envoys sent to negotiate with him. When the Emperor refused to release them, a small expedition commanded by Sir Robert Napier was sent to Abyssinia. The 1st Battalion of The King's Own and the 33rd Foot (later the 1st Battalion Duke of Wellington's Regiment), which were great rivals in India, had the leading roles in the campaign, the main feature of which was the epic march over roadless, mountainous country to Theodore's fortress at Magdala, 381 miles from the expedition's base at Zula on the Red Sea. The expedition started at the beginning of February and was in sight of Magdala on 6 April. On 10 April The King's Own, supported by artillery and Indian units, routed the Abyssinian Army at the Battle of Arogi. The 33rd Foot led the assault into Magdala on 13 April, whereupon Theodore committed suicide and the European prisoners were released. The return march began on 19th April and the 1st Battalion sailed from Zula on 2 June for Suez, landing at Dover on 23 June, where it received a civic reception. All ranks received the Abyssinian Campaign Medal. The Regiment was granted the Battle Honour ABYSSINIA.

The 1st Battalion remained in the south of England until 1874 and served at Gibraltar until 1879, before leaving for the West Indies. On 10 and 13 December 1878 the 2nd Battalion embarked for service in Natal during the Zulu War. Queen Victoria presented the Battalion with new Colours on 6 December, prior to its departure. The Battalion, much to its disappointment, spent the whole of the war guarding lines of communication, apart from a detachment which served as Mounted Infantry with Colonel Evelyn Wood's column, and saw action at the Battle of Inhlobana Hill, Kambula, and during the reconnaissance before the Battle of Ulundi. On 8 September 1879, after the main campaign was over, three companies of the Battalion took part in the attack on the caves of the Zulu Chief Manyanyoba, during which two NCOs were killed and one man wounded, probably the last casualties of the war. The Battalion embarked at Durban for Bombay on 8 February 1880. All ranks received the South Africa Medal, the majority with the date clasp '1879'. For its services during the Zulu War the Regiment was awarded the Battle Honour SOUTH AFRICA 1879.

The 1870s saw the introduction of a number of reforms to the British Army, which were brought about by the Minister of War, Edward Cardwell. These included the abolition of the purchase of officer's commissions, improvements in soldiers' pay and terms of engagement and organisation, and the allocation of a territorial connection to line infantry regiments.

Private Thomas Grady VC DCM, the first man in the Regiment to be awarded a Victoria Cross, for gallantry before Sebastopol in October and November 1854. Discharged to pension owing to wounds in October 1856, he received his Victoria Cross personally from Queen Victoria at a review in Hyde Park on 26 June 1857. He later emigrated to Australia and died near Melbourne in 1891. *Reproduced by kind permission of the Australian War Memorial, Canberra.*

PRIVATE THOMAS GRADY AND HIS COMRADE REPAIRING THE EMBRASURES UNDER A HEAVY FIRE FROM THE RUSSIAN BATTERIES.

A contemporary illustration of Private Tom Grady (with shovel) and his comrade Private Michael Regan repairing a gun embrasure under fire on 18 October 1854. Grady received the VC for the action and his comrade was recommended for the DCM with annuity. The 1st Battalion Digest records: 'On 19th January 1855 in consequence of a report respecting their distinguished conduct, the late Colonel Cobbe CB recommended No 3349 Pte Thomas Grady and No 3255 Patrick Regan for these distinctions. The Horse Guards authority granting the rewards was not received until 11th April 1855 Patrick Regan having died in the interim. A claim was subsequently made by No 1367 Michael Regan for some distinction on the grounds that he, and not Patrick Regan, had assisted in repairing the embrasure with Grady. Michael Regan's case having been substantiated by eye-witnesses he was recommended for the Victoria Cross, but did not obtain it.'

The British Army Camp before Sebastopol in 1855. According to the caption on the original photograph, the tents of the Light Division are on the left, the 2nd Division's huts in the centre and, beyond, the tents of the 4th Division. The tents and lines in the right foreground are noted as being those of the 4th Foot, on the edge of the 3rd Division's camp.

Mrs Elizabeth Evans with Chelsea Pensioners of the Regiment, including veterans of the Crimea, Indian Mutiny and Abyssinian and Zulu Campaigns, *circa* 1912. She married into the Regiment in 1852 and accompanied her husband to the Crimea, one of only 17 women to do so. Of the 17, only three, Mrs Evans, Mrs Rebecca Box and Mrs Chilton, went to the front. Mrs Evans remained with her husband until she fell ill with fever in late 1854 and was evacuated. After her husband's death she was given permission to wear his medals. She died on 30 January 1914 and was buried with full military honours, the only woman in the Regiment's history to be so honoured. Back row: Privates Mahoney, Manderville, Evans (no relation), Gosling and Knight. Front row: Private Hearsum, Mrs Evans and Private Smith.

Men of the 1st Royal Lancashire Militia outside Springfield Barracks, Lancaster, *circa* 1860. These Barracks, located at the top of Penny Street, were completed in 1855 and used until 1881, when the Regiment formed the 3rd and 4th Militia Battalions of The King's Own (Royal Lancaster Regiment) and moved to Bowerham Barracks. Prior to 1855 the Militia used various buildings in the town, including the Assembly Rooms as a Guard Room, the cells under the Town Hall for prisoners, the Castle for the Quartermaster's Stores and Armoury, and public houses for the soldiers' billets. After 1881, Springfield Barracks was used for a short time by the 5th Lancashire Artillery Volunteers and was then taken over by Storey Bros. The buildings are now occupied by Granada TV.

Lieutenant Henry Gregson of Lancaster wearing the early pattern grey uniform of the 10th Lancashire Rifle Volunteers (Lancaster), in 1861. The 10th was first raised in May 1859, and from 1876 it became the title of the Battalion which comprised Rifle Volunteer Companies from Fleetwood, Lancaster, Barrow, Ulverston, Hawkshead and Grange-over-Sands. The grey uniforms were worn until 1863, when they were replaced by scarlet tunics with blue facings.

Drum-Major Griggs with a drummer boy and band boys of the 2nd Battalion, Malta, 1865.

The encampment of the 2nd Battalion on the square at Floriana Barracks, Malta, during the cholera outbreak of 1865. The photograph, taken by Captain C. Breton, was published in the *Illustrated London News* of 28 October 1865. In the same month the Regiment had the distinction 'Royal' restored to its title, which had originally been granted in 1751.

Number 10 Company 2nd Battalion, Malta, 1865. This was the first of four postings to the island for the Regiment, the last being from August 1941 until October 1943 during the siege.

The Officers of the 2nd Battalion at the Depot at Parkhurst, Isle of Wight, in 1866. Standing on the right of the back row is Major James Paton who served in the Crimea, where he won the Legion of Honour. His nephew and grandson both served in the Regiment.

The 1st Royal Lancashire Militia parading on Giant Axe Field, Lancaster, on 22 May 1867. In the background is the approach to Lancaster Castle railway station, Lancaster Castle and the Priory Church. The Giant Axe Field, now the home of Lancaster City Football Club, was regularly used for parades by the Militia and subsequently by Battalions of The King's Own. These included the Regiment's 250th Anniversary celebrations in 1930, the 1st Battalion's Farewell Parade prior to amalgamation in 1959, and the presentation of new Colours to the 4/5th Battalion (TA) in 1962.

Officers of the 1st Battalion at Colaba Barracks, Bombay, in 1867, prior to embarking for Abyssinia. In the centre (standing, wearing cap and sword) is Brevet Colonel W. Wilby, who commanded a Brigade during the Campaign. To his left is Brevet Lieut-Colonel W. G. Cameron who commanded the Battalion. Both were awarded the CB for the Campaign and both became Colonels of the Regiment, Wilby from 1892 to 1894 and Cameron from 1894 to 1913.

Soldiers of the 1st Battalion inside King Theodore's fortress of Magdala, Abyssinia, April 1868. It was stormed on 13 April by the 33rd Foot (1st Battalion Duke of Wellington's Regiment) following the defeat of the Abyssinian Army at the Battle of Arogi on 10 April, fought on the plain below Magdala. The King's Own, the only British infantry unit to be involved in the engagement, used its newly-issued breech-loading Snider rifles with devastating effect against Theodore's troops. The Abyssinians suffered several hundred casualties, compared with the Regiment's one officer and seven other ranks wounded. The King's Own was ordered into Magdala on 15 April and spent three days destroying arms and stores.

Soldiers of the 1st Battalion on guard outside the church at Magdala, where King Theodore was buried, Abyssinia, April 1868.

Lieutenant H. C. Borrett (second from the left) with men of the 1st Battalion guarding the Kokit-Bur Gate at Magdala, April 1868. Lieutenant Borrett, who wrote a diary of events during the Campaign in a series of letters to his wife, later became a Major-General, received a CB, and had two sons and a grandson who served in the Regiment.

The troopship *Serapis* at Dover harbour disembarking soldiers of the 1st Battalion on their return from Abyssinia, 23 June 1868. The band, wearing white dress tunics, prepares to lead the Battalion from the quayside to the Citadel Barracks, where the Mayor and Corporation presented an illuminated address to the Regiment.

King Theodore's Drum. This silver drum was found at Magdala by Bandsmen of the 33rd Foot (1st Battalion Duke of Wellington's Regiment) on 13 April 1868. The 'Batta' officer ordered the drum to be returned, but following an appeal to Lord Napier by the 33rd's Colonel, it was divided into three. The 33rd received the centre section, and the 4th King's Own and 3rd Dragoon Guards one end each. The King's Own section, which is still held by the Officer's Mess of the 1st Battalion King's Own Royal Border Regiment, was traditionally worn over the neck and shoulder by a young subaltern when he took his first drink in the mess. Fortunately for the preservation of the drum, this practice has long since ceased. The photograph was taken in 1928 when the three sections of the drum were united for the first time since 1868.

The Abyssinian trophies of the 1st Battalion, 1895. When they returned from Abyssinia, the officers commissioned a silver centrepiece with their 'Batta' money (the share of the money from the proceeds of the sale of various items of booty taken during the Campaign). The centrepiece, known as 'Abyssinia', is reputed to be one of the tallest in the Army and was presented in 1875. It portrays Victory, cutting the chains of King Theodore's prisoners, standing on a plinth, the four sides of which depict scenes from the Campaign. Around the base, within laurel wreaths, are the Battle Honours of the Regiment up to 1868. The centrepiece and King Theodore's drum are still in use, as mentioned above. One of the shields and the silver-mounted beakers are in the Regimental Museum in Lancaster, and three of the four Coptic crosses are in the Regimental Chapel in Lancaster Priory and Parish Church (the fourth was stolen from the Chapel in 1980).

The Warrant Officers and Sergeants of the 1st Battalion at Anglesea Barracks, Portsmouth, about 1874. Most of the men are wearing their Abyssinia medals, including Quartermaster Sergeant Creedon (middle row, fifth from the right), who won the Distinguished Conduct Medal during the Campaign. Creedon's two sons and a grandson served in the Regiment — see pp 61, 126, 130 and 153.

Officers of the 2nd Battalion suitably attired for the Canadian weather at Wellington Barracks, Halifax, Nova Scotia, in March 1868. The Battalion spent two years in Halifax from 1866 to 1868. The officers' coats were of blue cloth with rolled collars and cuffs of grey sheepskin and were worn with black leather high boots and fur caps with a gold embroidered lion on the front.

A contemporary illustration of a riot at Mold, Flintshire, on 2 June 1869. A company of the 2nd Battalion under Captain Blake was sent from Chester Barracks to support the police, who were escorting two miners to the prison at Flint. The two men had been convicted of assault during a dispute between the miners and the Leeswood Coal Company. The police and soldiers were pelted with stones by a crowd of nearly 2,000 people as they escorted the prisoners from the courthouse to the station. The soldiers fired over the heads of the crowd but failed to disperse them; the magistrate then ordered them to fire at the crowd, of which five were killed and about 20 wounded. Two officers, 23 soldiers and a number of police were injured, some seriously. The Regiment was called upon to aid the Civil Power on many occasions in its history, but this is one of the few which involved fatalities. *Reproduced by kind permission of the Illustrated London News.*

THE RIOT AT MOLD, FLINTSHIRE: ATTACK ON THE SOLDIERS AT THE RAILWAY STATION.—SEE PAGE 601.

Queen Victoria presents new Colours to the 2nd Battalion at Windsor on 6 December 1878, shortly before it sailed to South Africa to take part in the Zulu War; the illustration appeared in *The Graphic* of 14 December 1878. The Colours are received by Lieutenants Shepherd and Hutchinson. Whilst serving with the mounted infantry during the Zulu War, Hutchinson was recommended for the Victoria Cross by Colonels Buller and Wood for saving the life of Private Garstin of the 2nd Battalion, when his horse was killed during a reconnaisance before the Battle of Ulundi in July 1879. The old Colours were placed in the Chapel at Windsor, but restored to the Regiment in July 1937 by the Earl of Athlone on behalf of King George VI.

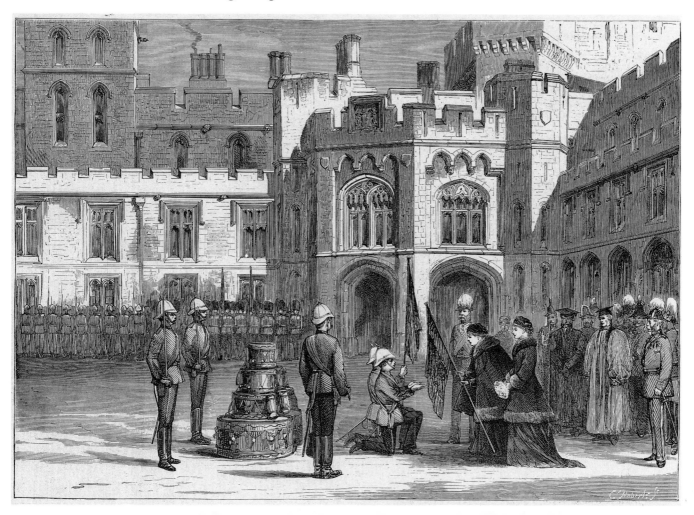

This is the only photograph in the Regimental archives of the 2nd Battalion in South Africa during the Zulu War in 1879. The group includes, from the left, Captain M. Crofton, Lieutenant Bonomi, Captain H. B. Laurence, the artist, and Captain H. Moore.

A contemporary sketch of the 2nd Battalion providing an escort to a convoy for Helpmakaar, Natal, during the Zulu War in 1879. It was drawn by Captain Henry Buckton Laurence (see above), a number of whose sketches were published by the *Illustrated London News*. During his career in the Regiment he produced drawings and paintings which included scenes in Canada 1866–8, the Irish Elections of 1868, and the Zulu War.

Chapter 3

1880-1899

THE REGIMENT COMES TO LANCASTER

The Regiment's connection with Lancaster resulted from one of the reforms instituted by Edward Cardwell, Minister of War. In the 1870s he introduced a territorial system whereby each of the country's ten military districts was sub-divided. To each sub-district area were assigned two regular infantry battalions, a militia and a volunteer regiment. Single-battalion regular infantry regiments were linked in pairs; one regular battalion from each district would always be serving overseas, kept up to strength by the other battalion in the United Kingdom, while the regimental depot, located in the sub-district, supplied the home battalion with trained recruits.

In 1873 Lancaster was chosen as the Headquarters of the 11th Brigade Sub-District, to which both Battalions of the 4th King's Own Royal Regiment, the 1st Regiment of Royal Lancashire Militia and the 5th (Administrative) Battalion Lancashire Rifle Volunteers were assigned. In April 1880 Bowerham Barracks, on the outskirts of Lancaster, became the Depot of The King's Own and its home for the next 79 years. In July 1881 the Sub-District was redesignated the 4th Regimental District and the Regiment re-titled The King's Own (Royal Lancaster Regiment). At the same time the two Battalions of the 1st Royal Lancashire Militia became the 3rd and 4th (Militia) Battalions of The King's Own, and their stores and personnel were

transferred from Springfield Barracks in the town. The new Depot had a permanent staff which was responsible for training both the regular recruits and those for the Militia. From 1880 onwards the Regiment attracted a large percentage of its recruits from the District area, which covered Lancashire north of Preston. In February 1883 the Rifle Volunteers were brought into the Regimental family as the 1st Volunteer Battalion, but had to wait until 1889 before they could wear The King's Own badge. By the turn of the century the 1st Volunteer Battalion had expanded to 12 companies and spread over an area extending from Fleetwood to the Furness District of Lancashire, with its headquarters in Ulverston.

Gradually the Regiment settled into its new home and by 1895 the area around the Barracks had developed as the Bowerham suburb of Lancaster. Soldiers became part of the local scene, whether on Church Parade, walking out, or on exercise on the barrack fields, and former members of the Regiment settled in the area on discharge from the Regular Army.

In 1880 the 1st Battalion was in the West Indies for the first time since 1826, companies being divided between Barbados, Trinidad and Jamaica. During the following year the detachment on Barbados was struck down by an epidemic of yellow fever, as a result of which 77 officers, men, women and children died. Between October 1881 and May 1882 the Battalion returned home, where it remained until being posted to Malta in 1894.

The 2nd Battalion went straight to India from South Africa in 1880 and was able to celebrate the Regiment's bi-centenary with a ball in Poona. The Battalion remained in India until December 1895, when it embarked for England. On its brief stop-over at Malta, men were transferred to the 1st Battalion and the officers and families of the two

Battalions met, a rare occurrence.

The new Austrian-pattern field service cap was introduced for wear in the Regiment, in 1894 for the NCOs and men and in 1896 for the officers. Initially the left-facing lion collar-badge, introduced for wear in 1872, was worn as the cap-badge, but in 1898 the new cap-badge, the lion with THE KING'S OWN underneath, was introduced in silver for officers, and brass for other ranks.

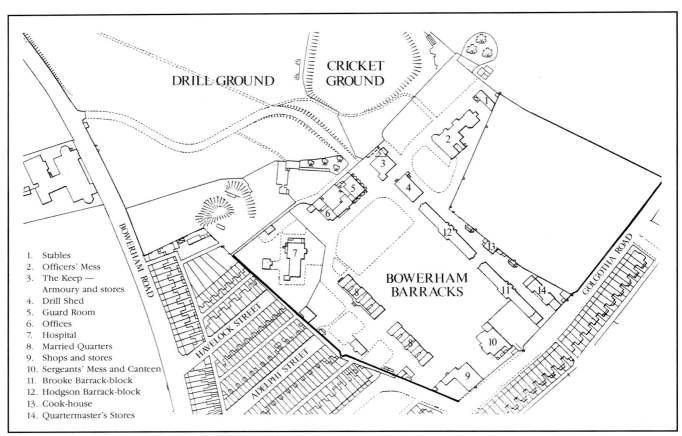

1. Stables
2. Officers' Mess
3. The Keep —
    Armoury and stores
4. Drill Shed
5. Guard Room
6. Offices
7. Hospital
8. Married Quarters
9. Shops and stores
10. Sergeants' Mess and Canteen
11. Brooke Barrack-block
12. Hodgson Barrack-block
13. Cook-house
14. Quartermaster's Stores

Plan of Bowerham Barracks, Lancaster, *circa* 1898, the Headquarters and Depot of the Regiment from 1880 until 1959. The site on the south side of Lancaster was originally charity land and was purchased in 1873 by the War Office for £7,300. The buildings took seven years to complete and in April 1880 the first Regimental staff moved in. Thereafter the layout of the buildings changed very little, although a miniature range, stores, new canteen and cook-house were added in the 1930s. Temporary wooden barracks and other buildings, built in 1939 on the Drill Ground, were used until after the war.

The Regiment's recruits were trained at Bowerham until August 1941, then until 1952, apart from a short period when the Depot was re-activated as a Primary Training Centre in 1946–7, recruit training was carried out at Carlisle. The training of National Servicemen resumed in 1952 and the last intake passed out in February 1959. The Depot closed officially on 26 September 1959.

The two soldiers' barrack-blocks at Bowerham were named Hodgson and Brooke. Three generations of the Hodgson family had been Colonels of the Regiment, whilst Lieutenant-Colonel Francis Brooke CB had commanded the 1st Battalion with distinction during the Napoleonic Wars. Each block contained four large barrack rooms on two floors, and here we see a barrack room in Hodgson block in 1897. Each soldier's kit and bed is laid out for the daily routine, with his locker under the bed. To the left of the fireplace is a large coal bucket. This scene hardly changed over the next 60 years (see pp108 and 158).

The combined band of the 3rd and 4th (Militia) Battalions photographed in front of the main entrance and keep at Bowerham Barracks, *circa* 1889. Several of the bandsmen are wearing the small lion collar-badges issued between 1881 and 1884. Drum-Major Foster's headgear is probably a reflection of artistic licence rather than regulation! Behind the group to the left is the Officers' Mess.

The band and cyclist section of the 1st Volunteer Battalion at annual camp on Lancaster Moor, July 1890. The Volunteers adopted the use of bicycles for patrol and reconnaissance work. The Territorial Battalions each retained a cyclist section until 1915 when they were absorbed into the Army Cyclist Corps.

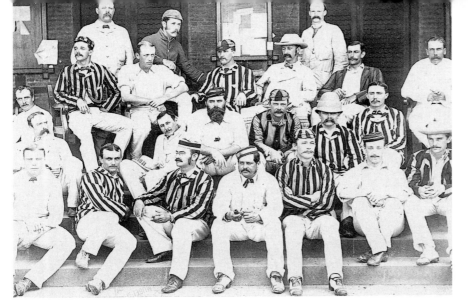

The all ranks cricket team of the 2nd Battalion, Karachi, India, in August 1888, following their defeat of Poona by an innings and 72 runs, and of Bombay by an innings and 20 runs. Note the wide variety of Regimental blazers, caps, ties and bow-ties. The 2nd Battalion had formed the Regiment's first cricket team at Poona four years earlier, although the earliest record of sport within the Regiment is in 1873, when the 1st Battalion held a sports day at Anglesea Barracks, Portsmouth.

The six-a-side soccer team of the 1st Battalion, Dublin, 1890.

Members of F Company (Ulverston) 1st Volunteer Battalion with their shooting trophies, 1894. In the centre is the 'Tilney Cup', the Company Championship Shooting Trophy of the Battalion. The cup later became an inter-Battalion shooting trophy of the 42nd East Lancashire Division (TA).

The Warrant Officers and Sergeants of the 2nd Battalion at Bombay, India, *circa* 1885; several are wearing their Zulu War medals. The Battalion arrived in India from South Africa in February 1880 and was stationed at Poona and Bombay before moving to Quetta on the North West Frontier in 1886, and later to Karachi, Hyderabad, Ahmednagar and Nasirabad.

Afternoon tea, Nasirabad, India, 1895. Captain C. A. Borrett, Mrs Kirk, Lieutenant A. R. Martin and Captain Kirk take tea. The native servants each wear a silver monogrammed Regimental badge on the turban.

The 1st Battalion trooping the Regimental Colour in the Palace Square, Malta, in 1897 during the Battalion's annual inspection. During its short stay on Malta from January 1896 to November 1897, the Battalion was quartered in the newly completed Imtarfa Barracks. The following year the Battalion held a formal St George's Day Parade and trooped the Regimental Colour. This is the first record of the Regiment celebrating its traditional day since 1705 at Gibraltar.

The cook-house and staff of the 2nd Battalion at Raglan Barracks, Devonport, 1897.

The Pioneers of the 2nd Battalion outside their workshops at Whittington Barracks, Lichfield, in 1898. Their role on active service was to keep the Battalion's line of march clear, but in barracks they were the joiners, carpenters and tradesmen of the Battalion. The soldier on the left carries an axe, the symbol of his trade, and on his belt wears the long-bladed, saw-backed bayonet issued to Pioneers. They were the only soldiers in the Battalion allowed to grow beards.

The 2nd Battalion's signal section at Whittington Barracks, Lichfield, January 1899.

The Officers' Mess silver of the 2nd Battalion, Whittington Barracks, Lichfield, January 1899. In the centre is 'Hebe', the centrepiece, purchased *circa* 1873 and still in use in the Officers' Mess of the 1st Battalion King's Own Royal Border Regiment. The figure, depicting the Greek Goddess Hebe carrying a wine flagon, was made *circa* 1837 in the workshops of the London silversmith Paul Storr. The sideboard had been presented by a former commanding officer, Colonel O. R. Middleton, at Bombay in 1885.

Major-General Sir Archibald Hunter, seated third from the left, with officers of the 2nd Battalion at Lichfield, 19 January 1899. A year later the 2nd Battalion, in the Lancashire Brigade of the 5th Division, was on active service trying to relieve the General and British forces besieged in Ladysmith. Others on the front row are Lieutenant and Adjutant A. M. Dykes (left), wounded on Spion Kop and killed in August 1914 in command of the 1st Battalion; Major Yeatherd (second from left), 2nd in command, killed at Pieter's Hill; and the Commanding Officer, Lieutenant-Colonel Malby Crofton (third from right), at 6 ft 8 in the tallest officer to serve in the Regiment.

Chapter 4
1899-1902
SOUTH AFRICA

Following the declaration of war on Britain by the Boer Republics on 11 October 1899, the two British Colonies in South Africa, Natal and Cape Colony, were invaded, and the towns and garrisons of Mafeking, Kimberley and Ladysmith besieged. Three Divisions were quickly formed in England and sent out to South Africa under the command of Sir Redvers Buller VC. In November the 2nd Battalion King's Own, based at Whittington Barracks in Lichfield, was mobilised and formed part of the 11th (Lancashire) Brigade, 5th Division. Reservists came in to the Depot at Lancaster and were sent to bring the Battalion up to strength, embarking for South Africa on the 30th. The British forces had in the meantime suffered defeats at Stormberg, Magersfontein and Colenso in their attempts to relieve the besieged towns.

The war was to affect all levels of the Regimental structure. On 14 December the 4th (Militia) Battalion was embodied and was one of the first Militia units to volunteer for overseas service. The offer was accepted and the Battalion sailed on 11 January 1900, having laid up its Colours in Lancaster Town Hall. The 3rd (Militia) Battalion was also embodied, laid up its Colours in Lancaster on 8 February and sailed on the 12th. The Volunteer Battalions (the 2nd was formed in 1900) provided the first of two Volunteer Service Companies attached to the 2nd Battalion. As each unit arrived and departed it received tremendous acclaim from the general public, who were gripped by a mixture of civic pride and patriotic enthusiasm. With the departure of both Militia Battalions on active service, the 1st Battalion was ordered back from Singapore in February 1900 to act as the drafting unit for the Battalions in South Africa.

During the course of the War almost 500 officers and men were sent out as reinforcements to the 2nd Battalion which, following its arrival in the Cape, joined Buller's forces in a second attempt to relieve the garrison at Ladysmith, which involved breaking through the Boer positions on the heights above the Tugela River. The Battalion took part in a series of actions from 20 January at Trichards Drift, Venter's Spruit, Spion Kop, Vaal Krantz and Onderbrook Hill until, on 28 February, the victory at Pieter's Hill finally opened up the road to Ladysmith. When the troops entered the town on 3 March to a tremendous reception, The King's Own saw General Hunter at the side of Sir George White and gave them a special cheer as they passed. The cost to the Battalion in these actions had been high, with 111 dead, 237 wounded and 28 taken prisoner.

Both the 3rd and 4th (Militia) Battalions were employed guarding lines of communication in Cape Colony and Orange Free State as Lord Roberts VC advanced to capture Bloemfontein,

Johannesburg and Pretoria. The 4th Battalion provided guards on the railway line in Cape Colony at the important junctions of Naauwpoort and De Aar from early February 1900, while the 3rd Battalion moved to Virginia Siding, on the Zand River north of Bloemfontein, in late May, remaining in the area until September 1901. Both Battalions saw little action and suffered the majority of their casualties through disease. However, in two isolated actions, the 3rd Battalion at Zand River Bridge on 14 June 1900 and the 4th Battalion at Fish River Station on 23 February 1901, both held out against superior Boer forces.

The 2nd Battalion remained in Natal and in late May 1900 formed the advance guard as the Army moved against Utrecht. It was present at the actions at Botha's Pass and Alleman's Nek on 8 and 11 June, which opened up routes through the Drakensberg Mountains. Laing's Nek, where the railway line from Ladysmith crossed into Transvaal, was occupied on the 12th.

On 11 December, several Companies of the 2nd Battalion successfully defended 'Lancaster Hill' near Vryheid against a determined Boer attack. For the remainder of the war the Battalion's role in northern Natal and the Transvaal was the guarding of lines of communication and the building and manning of the 'block-house' system, which formed barriers to prevent cross-country movement by the Boers.

In order to operate over long distances and deal with the widespread groups of Boers, mounted infantry units were formed; both the 2nd and 3rd Battalions formed detachments in 1900. From the beginning of 1901 the war entered into a phase of guerrilla warfare, until peace was signed on 31 May 1902. The use of mounted infantry then became essential since so many troops were tied down guarding strategic positions. In July 1900 the 1st Battalion started to train men for the mounted infantry units at Aldershot, the first of which arrived in January 1901. In all, nearly 450 officers and men from the 1st Battalion served with five Mounted Infantry Battalions from February 1901 until December 1902.

As each Battalion or unit returned home, it received a civic welcome. The first troops to return were the men of 1st Volunteer Service Company; both Lancaster and Barrow gave their own men civic receptions. The 4th and 3rd Militia Battalions received similar welcomes in Lancaster, as they paraded outside the Town Hall to receive back their Colours in August 1901 and February 1902. The 2nd Battalion, which did not return to England until March 1903, came up to Lancaster to collect its Colours, which had been laid up for the duration of the war in the Priory Church. The Regiment received the Battle Honours RELIEF OF LADYSMITH and SOUTH AFRICA 1899–1902 for service in South Africa. The Militia Battalions received separate Battle Honours for their Colours, SOUTH AFRICA 1900–02 for the 3rd and SOUTH AFRICA 1900–01 for the 4th.

The Mayor and Corporation of Lichfield present their gift of tobacco to the 2nd Battalion prior to its departure for South Africa, Whittington Barracks, November 1899.

The Warrant Officers and Sergeants of the 3rd (Militia) Battalion on the dockside at Southampton ready to sail on the SS *Majestic* for South Africa, 12 February 1900. RQMS Hardman (standing, front row, fourth from right), Sergeant Alcock (sitting on the right) and RSM Disley (standing, second from the left) were each awarded the Distinguished Conduct Medal during the Boer War. Both the 3rd and 4th Militia Battalions wore their scarlet tunics when they left England, which were exchanged for khaki on arrival at Cape Town.

The 1st Volunteer Service Company, formed from soldiers of the 1st Volunteer Battalion, parades on the square at Bowerham Barracks in March 1900. In all, two Companies and a Section were raised from the two Volunteer Battalions comprising men from Lancaster, Morecambe, Barrow, Ulverston, Millom, Dalton and Hawkshead. They went out to support the 2nd Battalion; the 1st Company left Lancaster on 16 March 1900 to great public acclaim and embarked for South Africa on the SS *Tagus* at Southampton.

The 2nd Battalion marching to Spion Kop, Natal, in January 1900. The photograph, sadly now damaged, was taken by the Reverend Hill, Chaplain to the Forces, Natal Field Force.

The British dead on Spion Kop, 25 January 1900, ready for burial in the front line trench where many of them were killed. The troops were only able to scrape a shallow trench in the rocky soil on the hilltop with their entrenching tools, as the picks and shovels had been left at the bottom of the hill, and this trench afforded little protection in the face of accurate Boer artillery and rifle fire from positions overlooking the hill. Most of these men were from The King's Own, Lancashire Fusiliers, South Lancashire Regiment and Thorneycrofts Mounted Infantry. The King's Own alone lost four officers and 48 other ranks killed, three officers and 90 other ranks wounded and one officer and 27 other ranks taken prisoner (later released). In addition, Major-General Sir E. R. P. Woodgate KCMG CB, a former King's Own officer commanding the Lancashire Brigade on Spion Kop, was also mortally wounded near this spot; he died on 23 March 1900 and is buried in St Paul's Churchyard, Mooi River. The British War Memorial stands at one end of the mass grave, and nearby is the Regimental War Memorial (right).

SPIONS KOP, NATAL. JAN 26TH, 1900.

Officers of the 3rd (Militia) Battalion at Cape Town, March 1900.

Mounted infantry of the 1st Battalion training at Aldershot for South Africa in March 1900; 444 officers and men from the 1st Battalion served in South Africa as Mounted Infantry during 1901 and 1902. The 1st Battalion sent out a further 496 officers and men as reinforcements for the 2nd Battalion during the war.

An accident on Botha's Pass, on the border between Natal and the Transvaal, 1900.

Lieutenant R. M. Luckcock carries out the rations inspection, 2nd Battalion, Dundee, Natal, late 1900. Luckcock later became a Major-General and was Colonel of the Regiment from 1945 to 1947.

Captain W. Mangles DSO and one of his guns on Lancaster Hill, Vryheid, Transvaal, 1900; several Companies of the 2nd Battalion defended this hilltop position against a superior Boer force in December 1900. Captain Mangles, who received his DSO for this action, was the son of Mr Ross Mangles, who won a civilian Victoria Cross during the Indian Mutiny when he took part in an expedition to relieve the town of Arrah near Dinapore, Bihar Province, in June 1857.

A work detail of the 2nd Battalion unloading railway line for repair work, Natal, May 1900. The Battalion helped to construct a diversion near Jakkalsfontein, where a bridge had been blown up by the Boers.

Armourer Sergeant Willcox, 4th (M) Battalion, with his field workshop, Naauwpoort, Cape Colony, 1900. Over 3,500 all ranks of the regiment who served in South Africa qualified for the Queen's South Africa Medal. The majority were awarded with one or more of the following clasps: Cape Colony, Natal, Tugela Heights, Orange Free State, Relief of Ladysmith, Transvaal, Laing's Nek, South Africa 1901 and South Africa 1902. Those men who were serving in South Africa on or after 1 January 1902, and who completed 18 months' service there before 1 June 1902, qualified for the King's South Africa Medal with the date bars South Africa 1901 and 1902. In addition the following decorations were awarded: one CB, one CMG and 14 DSOs to officers, and 20 DCMs to NCOs and other ranks of the Regiment.

Men of the 4th (M) Battalion striking camp at De Aar, Cape Colony, in 1900. De Aar was an important railway junction on the line between Cape Town and Kimberley.

Quartermaster Sergeant Moore, 4th (M) Battalion, with comforts from home, Naauwpoort, Cape Colony, 1900.

The 'garrison' with their pets at one of the 2nd Battalion's 'block-houses', De Jaagers Drift, Transvaal, April 1902.

Market Square, Lancaster, packed with crowds for the official welcome at the Town Hall for the Lancaster men of the 1st Volunteer Service Company, on their return from South Africa, 31 May 1901.

Chapter 5

1902-1914

STRENGTHENING TIES

The South African War had a tremendous impact not only on the British Army but also on the population of the country. Every Regiment in the Army had served in the war and Cardwell's territorial system had been put to the test. Increased public interest in The King's Own did much to create links with the communities in the Regimental area, which included an increasing number of men who had served or were serving in the Regiment, particularly those in the Militia and Volunteer Battalions. These ties were strengthened by events and changes in this period, which also had the effect of creating a greater sense of identity within the Regimental family.

In 1903 the foundation stone was laid for the Regimental Chapel. Built on to the north side of Lancaster Priory Church, it was dedicated to the dead of the Boer War. Completed in 1904, it provided not only a place of worship for officers and men of the Regiment, but also a suitable resting place for the Colours of various Battalions when taken out of use. In 1905 two stands of Militia Colours, and in 1906 the old 1st Battalion Colours, replaced the previous year and brought back from India, were laid up with great ceremony. The appointment of HM King Edward VII as Colonel-in-Chief of the Regiment was extremely popular, and the 1st Battalion later provided a party for his funeral procession in 1910. HM King George V

became the Regiment's Colonel-in-Chief in August 1913. The Regimental Magazine *The Lion and The Rose* was launched in 1905, and in 1912 the Regimental Old Comrades Association was formed.

The 1st Battalion, which had arrived in Malta in November 1901, continued its foreign service tour in India at Calcutta, Lebong, Shwebo (Burma) and Lucknow, before returning home to Dover at the end of 1912; in 1905 at Fort William, Calcutta, HRH the Prince of Wales presented it with new Colours. The 2nd Battalion came home from South Africa in 1903 to Blackdown Camp and was subsequently posted to Colchester, Jersey and Dover until 1912, when it sailed to India to replace the 1st Battalion. During this period training and sport within the Regiment received greater emphasis than ever before. Officers were encouraged to attend the Staff College, and officers and NCOs attended various other courses of instruction, particularly at the Small Arms School at Hythe. Soldiers were given the incentive of additional service pay from 1905 for improved proficiency.

Some of the most noticeable changes to affect the Regiment were the reforms introduced by Mr Haldane, the Secretary of State for War, to reorganise the Militia and Volunteer Battalions. In 1908, as a result of the Territorial and Reserve Forces Act 1907, the 4th (Militia) Battalion was disbanded, whilst the 3rd Battalion was redesignated the 3rd (Special Reserve) Battalion, and provided the nucleus of a third regular battalion. Recruits for the Special Reserve signed on for six years, undertook six months' training at the Regimental Depot, followed by short annual trainings, and were liable to service abroad in times of war. A permanent staff for the Battalion was based at the Depot.

The 1st and 2nd Volunteer Battalions respectively formed the 4th and 5th Battalions (Territorial Force) in 1908 and were brought up to strength with eight companies each. The Territorials were organised into Divisions to support the Regular Army, and in time of war each man would be paid at service rates and given six months' training if he volunteered for overseas service. The two King's Own Battalions formed the North Lancashire Brigade of the West Lancashire Division (TF). The 4th Battalion (TF) maintained its Headquarters and two Companies at Ulverston, with other Companies at Barrow-in-Furness, Dalton and Millom. The 5th Battalion (TF) had its headquarters and four Companies in Lancaster, with Companies at Morecambe, Carnforth and Fleetwood. The Territorial Force became very popular, since for many of these part-time soldiers it provided the opportunity, at weekend trainings and annual camp, to go away from home. In Lancaster three of the Companies were formed entirely from the workforces of Storey Bros and James Williamson and Son.

The interior of the Regimental Chapel in Lancaster Priory and Parish Church, photographed in 1948. The foundation stone was laid on 7 August 1903 by Constance, Countess of Derby, and the Chapel was dedicated by the Bishop of Manchester on 29 July 1904. A Memorial Brass to those who had fallen during the Boer War and a stained-glass window in memory of Lieutenant-Colonel Gawne, killed at Vryheid in December 1900, were unveiled by Field-Marshal Lord Roberts VC on the same day. The chapel was the first of its kind in England and was designed by Messrs Austin and Paley, Architects, of Lancaster. Part of the original north wall of the nave was moved outwards, the wall being connected to the body of the church by an apse at the east end and by a west wall. Four arches and oak screens separate the chapel from the nave.

The Chapel was originally built as a memorial to those who had died on active service in South Africa during 1900–1902. On the left is the memorial to HM King Edward VII and above that a replica of his bannerette. Old Colours of the Regiment, the most recent at the far end, hang in the roof. Memorial plaques are mounted on the walls and smaller brass plaques in memory of former officers of the Regiment and the Regiment's VC winners are fastened to the ends of the oak pews and panelling. The fixtures, furniture and pews in the chapel have all been presented from time to time in memory of former officers. At the far end on the right is the bronze casket containing the Rolls of Honour for the First and Second World Wars. It was the duty of a soldier from the Regimental Depot and later from the TA Battalion to turn the page of the Roll every Sunday. This duty is now performed on the first Sunday of the month by a member of the Regimental Association.

'Body-builders' of the 1st Battalion, Aldershot, 1901.

The 1st Battalion's team which won the Pembroke Camp Challenge Cup at the Malta Rifle Meeting in 1902. Back row, left to right: C/Sgt T. G. Creedon, Sgt A. Creedon, C/Sgt A. W. Morrell; centre: Maj G. L. Hibbert DSO, Capt J. H. Lloyd; front row: C/Sgt R. Fitton, 2/Lt W. B. Somerville and Cpl E. W. Morrell. All of these officers and men had family links with the Regiment spanning several generations.

Lance-Corporal Culbert, A Company 1st Battalion, with his kit laid out for inspection, Malta, March 1902.

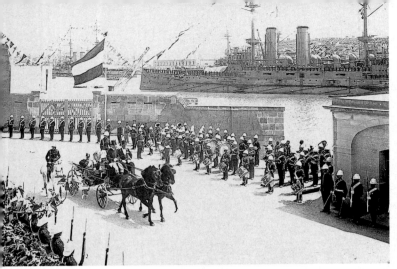

King Edward VII passes soldiers and the band of the 1st Battalion on his arrival in Malta on 14 April 1903. During this visit, on 17 April, the King announced his intention of becoming Colonel-in-Chief of the Regiment. Following the inspection of the Guard-of-Honour provided by the Battalion at the Customs House for his departure on 21 April, His Majesty commented: 'It has given me great pleasure to see so fine a Guard furnished by the Regiment with which I now have the honour to be permanently associated.'

On 14 July 1905 the 3rd and 4th (Militia) Battalions received new Colours from the King, Colonel-in-Chief of the Regiment, at Knowsley, home of Lord Derby, honorary Colonel of the 4th Battalion. His Majesty presented the King's Colour of the 3rd Battalion to Second Lieutenant Stokes; Second Lieutenant Linton received the Regimental Colour. The Derby family had a long and close association with the Regiment — Lord Derby had served in the 3rd Militia Battalion, was Honorary Colonel of the 4th Militia Battalion (1886–1908) and later the 5th Battalion (TA) (1932–1947). His grandson presented new Colours to the 4/5th Battalion (TA) in 1962 and maintains close links with the present 4th (Volunteer) Battalion of The King's Own Royal Border Regiment.

The Colour Party of the 5th (Territorial) Battalion in the Drill Hall, Phoenix Street, Lancaster, with the new Colours presented by King Edward VII at a review of the West Lancashire Territorial Division on 5 July 1909. The King presented new Colours to eight of the 12 Battalions on parade, including the 4th and 5th Battalion King's Own. From left to right: C/Sgt Ralph, Lt Atkinson (King's Colour), C/Sgt Gardner, Lt W. O. Wright (Regimental Colour), C/Sgt Hughes. The Phoenix Street Drill Hall was built for the Lancaster Companies of the 1st Volunteer Battalion circa 1895. From 1900 it became the Headquarters of the 2nd Volunteer Battalion and from 1908 of the 5th Battalion (TF). The buildings were used by the Territorial Army until 1990, when Alexandra Barracks on Caton Road in Lancaster, the new Headquarters of the 4th (Volunteer) Battalion King's Own Royal Border Regiment, was opened on 12 July by HRH Princess Alexandra, the Regiment's Colonel-in-Chief.

The 1st Battalion Rugby XV, winners of the Calcutta Rugby (open to India) Tournament Challenge Cup, India, 1904.

A team of the 2nd Battalion competing in the Evelyn Wood Marching Competition through the village of Runfold, near Aldershot, in 1906. The competition comprised a speed march followed by target shooting.

The front page of the first edition of the Regimental magazine *The Lion and The Rose*, which was introduced in 1905. It was published and edited in India by the 1st Battalion, until its return to England in 1912, when the paper was transferred to the Depot. It was published monthly for the first three years then quarterly until 1914, and from January 1921 until October 1959. It was succeeded by *The Lion and The Dragon*, the Regimental magazine of The King's Own Royal Border Regiment.

The wedding group for the marriage of Lieutenant L. I. Cowper (seventh officer from the left) at the Garrison Church, Calcutta, 1 February 1906. Cowper retired in 1935 as a Lieutenant-Colonel after 35 years' service, having commanded the Regimental Depot and the 5th Battalion (TA). His lasting memorial is the Regimental history, of which he edited the first two volumes (1680–1914), published in 1939. The third volume (1914–1950) was completed by his daughter, Colonel Julia Cowper TD WRAC, and published in 1957.

The shoemakers' shop of the 1st Battalion, Shwebo, Burma, *circa* 1906. These soldiers, who were qualified tradesmen, were responsible for the upkeep and repair of the Battalion's footwear, leather equipment and harness.

The Band of the 1st Battalion, winners of the Mandalay Rugby Merchant Shield and Regimental Football Shield, Shwebo, Burma, 1907.

A corner of H Company 2nd Battalion's barrack-room, Goojerat Barracks, Colchester, 1907.

The 'Far West' as presented by men of the Depot at a Bowerham Barracks garden fete in July 1907. This fete, organised to raise funds for the Regimental Chapel, was one of the first events at the Barracks open to the public. In the middle distance the half-completed Ashton Memorial can just be seen.

The 2nd Battalion Trooping the Colour on St George's Day 1909, at Fort Regent, Jersey.

Drum-Major J. Coney, 1st Battalion, Lucknow, India, 1910. He is wearing the old-style forage-cap with bullion wire lion and rose badges. These caps had largely disappeared from use with the introduction of the Austrian-pattern field service caps *circa* 1896.

The 1st Battalion parading in review order, Lucknow, 1910. The Battalion is drawn up in its eight rifle companies with the officers at the front. On the left are the Band and Drums with the machine-gun section behind.

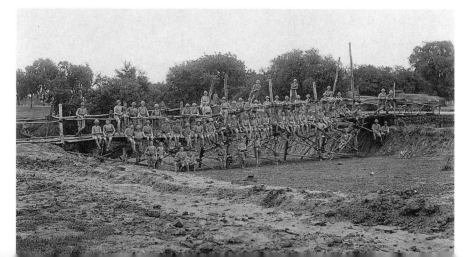

Bridge builders, E Company 1st Battalion, Lucknow, 1911.

The 4th Battalion (TF) marching out for the day's exercise at annual camp, Hornby, near Lancaster, 1910.

HM King George V inspects a Guard-of-Honour provided by the 5th Battalion (TF) in Dalton Square, Lancaster, on 24 August 1912. His Majesty is accompanied by Brigadier-General North CB MVO and Lieutenant-Colonel Lord Richard Cavendish, the Commanding Officer. The following year the King became the Regiment's Colonel-in-Chief.

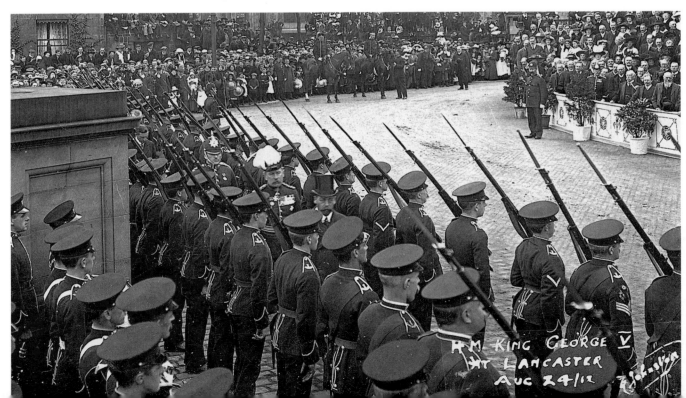

The inaugural dinner of The King's Own Old Comrades Association at the Birkbeck Cafe, London, on 20 April 1912.

Officers of the 1st Battalion who attended a Levee at St James's Palace on 12 June 1913. Back row, left to right: Capt W. Somerville, 2/Lt R. Matthews, Lt G. Blackburn, Lt A. S. Pott DCM, 2/Lt C. Irvine, Lt C. Steele-Perkins; middle row: 2/Lt E. Burke, Lt C. Carter, 2/Lt W. Statter, Lt L. Woodgate, Lt & Adjt T. Uzielli, Lt G. Keith; front row: Capt L. I. Cowper, Lt Col T. Marker, Gen Sir A. Hunter GCB GCVO DSO, Capt C. Grover and Capt H. Clutterbuck. General Sir Archibald Hunter GCB GCVO DSO TD LLD FRGS (1856–1936) (see page 48), known to all ranks as 'Archie', was one of the most brilliant officers of his time. Gazetted to the Regiment from Sandhurst in 1874 aged 17, he served in the Egyptian Army from 1884 to 1899, seeing action in numerous campaigns in the Sudan and holding Governorship of the Red Sea littoral and of Dongola Province. For his services at the final battle of Atbara and Omdurman he received the thanks of Parliament and a KCB. In May 1899 he assumed command of the Quetta Division in India, but joined the Natal Field Force in South Africa as Chief-of-Staff to Sir George White VC. He served at the Defence of Ladysmith and, as a Lieutenant-General, led remarkably successful drives against the Boers before returning home through illness. Following commands in Scotland and India, and promotion to General, he became Governor and Commander-in-Chief of Gibraltar (1910–13); Commander-in-Chief Aldershot Command (1914–17); and Aide-de-Camp to HM King George V (1917). He was Colonel of The King's Own (1913–26), MP for Lancaster (1918–22), and a Freeman of the town.

The Cyclist Section of the 5th Battalion (TF) at annual camp, Denbigh, North Wales, 1913.

The Drums of the 1st Battalion at the Citadel Barracks, Dover, 1913.

Chapter 6

1914-1919

THEY WIN OR DIE WHO WEAR THE ROSE OF LANCASTER

At the outbreak of war in August 1914 the Regiment comprised two Regular, two Territorial and a Special Reserve Battalion. By the war's end it had expanded to 17 Battalions, ten of which saw active service. During the war over 4,000 officers and 41,000 other ranks served in the various Battalions, of which 298 officers and 6,143 other ranks were killed, or died as a result. Indeed, the latter total is probably closer to 7,000, allowing for those who died as a result of wounds after the war and former members of the Regiment who were killed whilst serving with other units. The effect on the towns and villages within the Regimental area and Lancashire as a whole paralleled that elsewhere in the country, the War Memorials providing a permanent reminder of the colossal sacrifice.

The 1st Battalion was mobilised on 4 August 1914, was rapidly made up to strength with reservists from the Regimental Depot at Lancaster, and embarked for France with the 12th Infantry Brigade of the 4th Division on 22 August, spending the whole of the war on the Western Front. The 2nd Battalion in India returned home, joined the 83rd Infantry Brigade of 28th Division and left for the Western Front where it served from January until November 1915, when it moved to Salonika.

Both the 4th and 5th Battalions (TF) were mobilised in August, and a large proportion of the officers and men volunteered for overseas service. They were initially employed on home defence before leaving for the Western Front to support units in other divisions until their own 55th (West Lancashire) Division was reformed in France in 1916. The 4th Battalion left England in May 1915 and the 5th in mid-February 1915. The Territorials were also able to raise second and third line Battalions in 1914 and 1915 and on doing so the two original Battalions were redesignated the 1/4th and 1/5th Battalions (TF). Of the second and third line units, only the 2/5th Battalion went overseas to the Western Front in the 170th Brigade of 57th Division (TF) on 5 February 1917. The other Battalions were in 1916 combined to form the 4th Reserve Battalion to supply reinforcements.

The 3rd (Special Reserve) Battalion was mobilised in August 1914 and during the war processed thousands of trained men for the Regular and Service Battalions overseas, including men returning from convalescence. By mid-1915 the Battalion was based near Plymouth, where it remained until the end of the war. Two other Reserve Battalions, the 10th and 12th (TF), were also raised.

As a result of Lord Kitchener's appeal for 100,000

men, the Regiment rapidly formed four Battalions for the New Army, the 6th, 7th, 8th and 9th. Initially raised in Lancaster, they were quickly dispersed to the south and south-west of England to be trained. The 6th (Service) Battalion joined the 38th Infantry Brigade of 13th (Western) Division and sailed for Gallipoli in June 1915; from February 1916 until the end of the war it fought in Mesopotamia (Iraq). The 7th (Service) Battalion joined the 56th Infantry Brigade of 19th Division and served on the Western Front from July 1915 until disbandment in February 1918, when its personnel were transferred to the 1/4th and 1/5th Battalions (TF). The 8th (Service) Battalion served with 25th and 3rd Divisions on the Western Front from September 1915 until the Armistice. The 9th (Service) Battalion joined the 122nd Brigade of 22nd Division, served briefly in France then subsequently in Salonika (Macedonia) and Bulgaria.

The last unit of the Regiment to be raised for active service was the 11th (Service) Battalion in June 1915. This was a 'Bantam' Battalion, so-called because it accepted men below the official height requirement and included a large number of miners from the central Lancashire coalfields. It joined the 120th Brigade of 40th (Bantam) Division and served in France and Flanders from June 1916 until disbandment in February 1918.

The Regiment participated in most of the major engagements of the war, particularly in France and Flanders. The 1st Battalion suffered nearly 400 casualties near Le Cateau on 26 August 1914, within four days of arriving in France. It also took part in the Battles of the Marne and Aisne and the first Battle of Ypres in 1914. The 1st, together with the 2nd and 1/5th Battalions, fought in the second Battle of Ypres in May 1915. On 8 May near Frezenberg, the 2nd Battalion suffered over 900 casualties, which included more than 300 killed or died of wounds. The 2nd Battalion was again in action, together with the 7th, at the Battle of Loos in September 1915. The 8th Battalion fought with distinction at the Bluff and St Eloi in March-April 1916, while five Battalions, the 1st, 1/4th, 1/5th, 7th and 8th, fought on the Somme later in the year.

On 1 July 1916 the 1st Battalion suffered heavy casualties, including its Commanding Officer, Major Bromilow, who was killed in the attack on German positions at Beaumont Hamel. In contrast, the 7th Battalion was able to capture La Boisselle to the south on 3 July with relatively few casualties. The 1st Battalion distinguished itself at Arras in April-May 1917 during the First Battle of the Scarpe. The 7th Battalion also fought at the successful attack on Messines Ridge in June 1917 and, with all the other Battalions of the Regiment on the Western Front, took part in the third Battle of Ypres, including the actions at Polygon Wood, Broodseinde, Poelcappelle and Passchendaele. In late March 1918, during the German Spring Offensive, the 1st Battalion fought in the defence of Arras at the Battle of the Scarpe. At Givenchy on 9 April, the 55th (West Lancashire) Division (TF), which included the 1/4th and 1/5th Battalions, stubbornly held on to their positions. The 1st, 1/4th, 1/5th, 2/5th and 8th Battalions all participated in the heavy fighting during August and September 1918 which broke through the Hindenburg Line.

Meanwhile, the 6th Battalion had remained in the Middle East. At Gallipoli it served at Cape Helles, Anzac Bay, where it saw heavy fighting in August 1915, and finally at Suvla Bay. The Battalion was one of the last to leave the area during the evacuation of the Gallipoli Peninsula, and from February 1916 it fought in Mesopotamia as part of the force attempting to relieve the besieged garrison of Kut-al-Amara. Both the 2nd and 9th Battalions fought in Salonika (Macedonia) against the Bulgarians and had to cope with the rugged country, extremes of cold and heat in winter and summer and regular bouts of malaria.

After the Armistice the various Battalions were carrying out duties in occupied territories. The 1st, 1/4th, 1/5th, 2/5th and 8th Battalions were in Germany, the 2nd and 9th Battalions in Greece and Turkey and the 6th in the Middle East. Between June and December 1919 each Battalion, reduced to Cadre strength, returned to England. The exception was the 1/5th Battalion, which travelled to the Curragh in Ireland; its Cadre returned to Lancaster in mid-October.

The Regiment was awarded 59 Battle Honours for the First World War. Amongst the many decorations for gallantry awarded to all ranks were eight Victoria Crosses, three of them posthumous.

The 5th Battalion (TF) leaves its billets, the disused Wagon Works on Caton Road, Lancaster, to march up to the Castle Station where it entrained for Didcot on 14 August 1914. The Battalion had gone to camp at Kirkby Lonsdale on 2 August, but returned to Lancaster on the 3rd, was mobilised on the 5th and was sent to Barrow to guard the docks and roads. It had returned to Lancaster on the 12th.

Fleetwood Reservists/ Territorials gather in the town's Market Hall on mobilisation in August 1914.

Led by Major Bates, the second-in-command of the 5th Battalion (TF), the Lancaster Pals march down Castle Park, Lancaster, after Church Parade at St Mary's Priory and Parish Church on 11 September 1914. The straw hats appear to be the only standard items of clothing. This Pals Company of over 200 men was raised in a matter of hours on 2 September to replace men too old, or medically unfit, to proceed overseas with the 5th Battalion. Dubbed the 'Gallant 200' by the *Lancaster Observer,* the group briefly trained in Lancaster before joining the Battalion at Didcot.

A company of the 4th Battalion (TF) outside the Battalion Headquarters, Ulverston Drill Hall, in 1914. The Drill Hall, originally built for the Lancashire Rifle Volunteers by public subscription and opened in 1873, was used by the Volunteers and Territorials until 1967.

Lieutenant-Colonel A. M. Dykes, who was killed whilst commanding the 1st Battalion at Haucourt near Le Cateau on 26 August 1914, within four days of arriving in France. On that morning the Battalion was caught in the open on a forward slope, with arms piled, by artillery and heavy machine-gun fire and suffered over 400 casualties. A recruit at the Regimental Depot in 1940 recalled being told that after this action the order 'pile arms' was never again given when the Regiment was on active service. Lt-Col Dykes has no known grave and is commemorated on the La Ferte Memorial.

Lieutenant R. C. Matthews in the 1st Battalion's forward trench at St Marguerite near Venizel, during the advance to the Aisne in September 1914. The trench is fairly shallow, simply reinforced and affords little protection against shell fire in contrast to the defences built later in the war. *IWM Q51499*

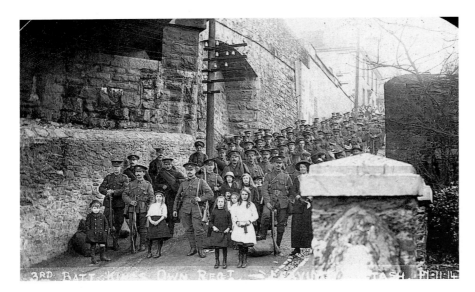

A group of the 3rd (Special Reserve) Battalion at Saltash on 17 November 1914 prior to entraining for Sunderland, Co Durham, where the Battalion was based until mid-1915.

Reservists of the 5th Battalion (TF) outside the YMCA building on China Street, Lancaster, in September 1914. There was no shortage of recruits for the Lancaster Territorials, who were soon able to form 2nd and 3rd Battalions. Several of the men are wearing blue and orange silk ribbons (the Regimental colours) on their left shoulders. These were presented by the Mayor and Mayoress of Lancaster in the absence of any available cap-badges or insignia.

The Barrow motor lorry, which the 1/5th Battalion (TF) used to draw rations from Abingdon and Oxford, at Didcot in 1914. Regimental Quartermaster Sergeant Woodcock is sitting in the front on the right.

Dr Bill George of Lancaster, the 1/5th Battalion (TF)'s Medical Officer, inoculates Sergeant Clarkson at Sevenoaks in January 1915. Dr George was commissioned in 1913 into the RAMC and won the MC during the war. He was the 5th Battalion's Medical Officer from 1921 until 1938, received the Territorial Decoration and retired as a Colonel.

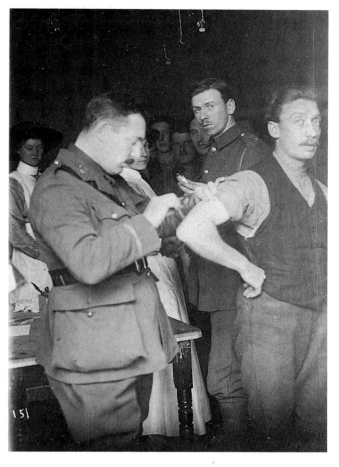

A group of the 1/5th Battalion (TF) on guard duties on the Great Western Railway line between Didcot and Oxford. Both first-line Territorial Battalions furnished these guards along a 50-mile section of line from mid-August to early November 1914 and, through accidents, suffered their first fatalities of the war.

Private Billy Poole (right) from Little Urswick, Ulverston, and comrade of the 8th (Service) Battalion. The photograph, probably taken in September 1914, shows them wearing the 'Blue' uniforms prior to the issue of khaki. Both men wear the small white enamel lapel badges embossed '8 K.O.R.', which were issued to men of the Battalion before cap-badges and shoulder titles became available. Billy Poole was killed aged 23 on 20 October 1915 at Sanctuary Wood, Hooge, near Ypres, and is buried in the Divisional Cemetery, Dickebusch Road, Vlamertinghe, Belgium.

The cook-house detail of the 9th (Service) Battalion at Aldershot in late 1914, under the charge of Sergeant Charles Williams, a former regular with the 1st Battalion.

The 'Spud Bashers' of the 1/5th Battalion (TF) at the Corn Exchange, Didcot, in September 1914. The cook-house and Quartermaster's store were based here.

Practise for things to come. Trench-digging at Sevenoaks by the 1/5th Battalion (TF) in late 1914. The Battalion left for France on 14 February and was re-placed by the 2/5th Battalion (TF), which had been based at Blackpool.

Men of the 7th (Service) Battalion training with dummy wooden Vickers machine-guns at a 56th Infantry Brigade machine-gun class, Clevedon, Somerset, in early 1915.

Corporal Cranney (left) and accomplice conduct a concert party of B Company, 7th (Service) Battalion, at Clevedon early in 1915. Although clothed in khaki, some of the men lack cap-badges and all wear the obsolete Boer War period Slade-Wallace equipment.

C/Sgt F. C. Lelliot, 1st Battalion, and his wife Maude after their wedding at Southsea on 16 January 1915. Promoted to CSM on his return to Belgium, he was awarded the DCM and Gold Medal of the Russian Order of St George for sustained gallantry and good work during the winter of 1914-15. He was killed in action near Ypres on 24 May 1915 and is commemorated on the Menin Gate Memorial at Ypres.

The Officers' Mess kitchen of the 2nd Battalion at Ouderdom near Ypres, February 1915. Second from the right is Sergeant Brockman; the soldier on the left wears a goatskin jacket. The Battalion's wooden huts can be seen in the background.

B Company, 2nd Battalion, on parade at Dranoutre in March 1915.

A Group of B Company 2nd Battalion in the trenches near Zonnebeke, Ypres Salient, April 1915. Sergeant Clarkson is on the left. Several of the men have removed their cap-badges.

Shelter in the trenches at Zonnebeke for the 2nd Battalion in April 1915. Note the rum bottle in the foreground.

The convoy of London buses transporting the 1/5th Battalion (TF) to the front from Winnizeele to Bailleul, Northern France, on 2 March 1915.

Men of the 1/5th Battalion (TF) in their trench, Ypres Salient in May 1915.

Sergeant Streeton and the cook-house staff of 1/5th Battalion (TF) with the roast out of the ovens near Ypres Salient in 1915. These 'Dutch ovens' were made out of clay/mud with a chimney. They were fired up and then sealed when the tray of meat or bread, etc, was inside. The residual heat cooked the food in a similar way to a slow cooker.

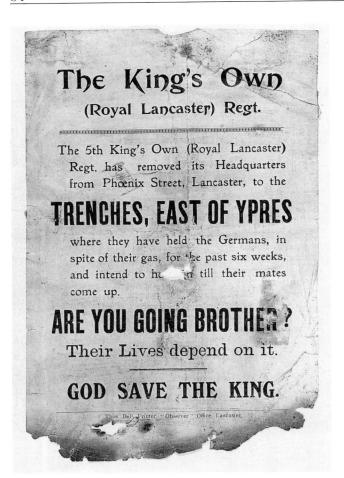

A recruiting handbill for the 5th Battalion (TF) printed in Lancaster in the spring of 1915.

The first gas helmets issued to the 1/5th Battalion (TF), Belgium, June 1915.

**Private Carr, Private Thompson and Sergeant Clowes
of the 1/5th Battalion (TF) cleaning up the trenches at
Loos, winter 1915.**

**Captain T. C. Owtram, Lieutenant J. J. Gilchrist, Captain W. N. Briggs and Lieutenant E. R. Simpson in the 1/5th
Battalion's trenches at Loos in late 1915. All of these officers survived the war, Owtram being awarded an MC,
Gilchrist and Briggs being mentioned in despatches. Both Gilchrist and Simpson were commissioned from the
ranks, having volunteered in September 1914.**

A group of the 3/4th (Reserve) Battalion (TF) at Weeton near Blackpool in 1915; the 3/4th and 3/5th Battalions (TF) were raised in June 1915 and based at the resort. In January the 2/4th Battalion (TF) amalgamated with the 3/4th and in April moved to Oswestry where it absorbed the 3/5th to become the 4th Reserve Battalion. It remained at Oswestry for the duration of the war, providing drafts of men for various Battalions of the Regiment.

The Warrant Officers and Sergeants of the 6th (Service) Battalion at Blackdown Camp near Farnborough, Hants, in June 1915.

An advert in the *Lancaster Guardian* in July 1915 for the raising of the 11th (Service) Battalion, the last of the Kitchener units of the Regiment to be formed.

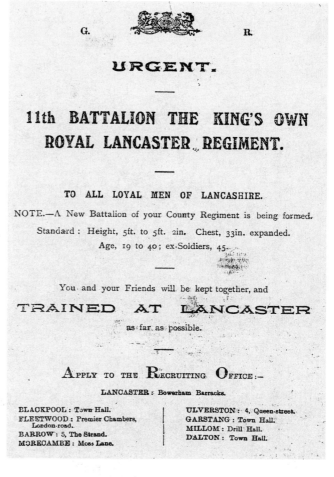

The 7th (Service) Battalion marching through a village near Calonne, France, in the late summer of 1915. *IWM Q17336*

Lance-Corporal H. Martin, 1/4 Battalion (TF), following the presentation of his DCM for capturing a German Officer and three other Germans single-handed on the night of 8–9 September 1915. He has also been promoted to Corporal, the new stripes just tacked on to his tunic. Martin, a former regular soldier in the Regiment, had enlisted in the Territorials in 1913, and his appearance and expression typify the strain on the fighting soldier.

A group from A Company, 1st Battalion, in their front line trench on Hawthorn Ridge near Beaumont Hamel, Somme, on 30 August 1915. The Battalion attacked the German front line in this area on 1 July 1916, when ten officers including Major Bromilow, the Commanding Officer, were killed, and 12 wounded. There were 387 other ranks casualties out of the 507 who went over the top.

Private Harry Christian, 2nd Battalion, of Ulverston, receives his Victoria Cross from HM King George V in Glasgow in September 1917. Christian, a pre-war regular soldier, won his VC for digging out under fire three comrades buried by a shell at Givenchy on 18 October 1915 (see Appendix 4). He was subsequently wounded, but later rejoined his Battalion in Salonika in 1918.

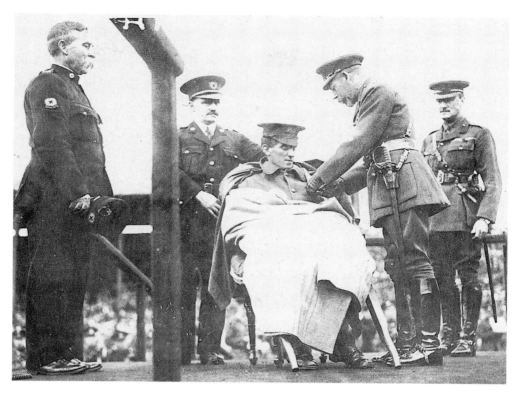

King's Own prisoners-of-war in Fredricks Feld POW Camp, Germany, *circa* 1916. During the war, funds for the relief of Regimental prisoners-of-war were established; Mrs H. Wilson of Lancaster and Miss Fell of Ulverston, for example, ran funds to provide food parcels for men of the 2nd and 1/4th Battalions. A Regimental Care Committee, based at the Regimental Depot, dealt with clothing parcels for prisoners of all Battalions and food parcels for all except the 2nd and 1/4th Battalions. Over 64,000 food and nearly 8,000 clothing parcels were distributed, from the £46,000 collected during the war.

11TH. (SERVICE) BATTN. THE KINGS OWN (R.L.R.) BLACKDOWN BARRACKS, JUNE 1916. ON PARADE FOR INSPECTION BY GENERAL SIR A. HUNTER BEFORE PROCEEDING TO FRANCE.

The 11th (Service) Battalion parades at Alma Barracks, Blackdown Camp, near Farnborough, Hampshire, prior to leaving for France on 2 June 1916.

Private James Miller VC (fourth from the right, back row) with his platoon of the 7th (Service) Battalion at Lucknow Barracks, Tidworth, probably in June 1915 before the Battalion left for the Western Front. The Battalion was based at Tidworth from 27 March to 16 June 1915. Miller was awarded a posthumous Victoria Cross for carrying a vital message under fire and returning with the reply despite being mortally wounded, near Bazentin-le-Petit on the Somme on 30 July 1916 (see Appendix 4). On Miller's right are Privates E. Snape and J. Marsden, both colleagues from the Wiggins Teape Paper Mill at Withnell near Chorley where they worked before the war.

A carrying party of the 1/4th Battalion (TF), laden with picket spikes and sandbags, walk along a support trench on the Somme in late 1916. Soldiers of all Regiments spent a great deal of time on mundane duties, which included carrying, wiring parties and digging trenches. *Taylor Library*

A platoon of the 1/4th Battalion (TF) on the Somme in 1916 — there are very few photographs of the Regiment in front line areas from 1916 until the end of the war. It is interesting to note that after over a year in France the soldiers are still using Long Lee-Enfield rifles. *Taylor Library*

The 2/5th Battalion (TF) march-past during a review of the 57th West Lancashire Division (TF) by HM King George V at Aldershot in September 1916.

Private Jack White VC, 6th (Service) Battalion. White won his Victoria Cross for saving the life of his officer during an attempting crossing of the River Dialah in Mesopotamia (Iraq) on the night of 7–8 March 1917 (see Appendix 4).

Private F. Sedgebeer from Halton near Lancaster with Lewis gun and comrade of the 6th (Service) Battalion in Mesopotamia in 1917. This is one of the few photographs taken of the Battalion on active service.

The dug-outs of the 2nd Battalion's Headquarters at Minden Terrace, Doiran Front, Salonika, in May/June 1917.

A soldier of the 2nd Battalion with captured donkeys and Bulgarian MG equipment after a raid on Bursute, in the Struma Valley, Salonika, on 25 February 1918.

Lance-Sergeant Tom F. Mayson, 1/4th Battalion (TF). He was awarded the Victoria Cross for destroying two enemy machine-gun positions and holding an isolated position until ordered to withdraw at Wieltje, Belgium, on 31 July 1917 (see Appendix 4).

Private Albert Halton VC (seated on the left) with comrades of the 1st Battalion, including Pte Tom Wilkson MM of Ulverston (standing on the right), at Arras in 1917. Halton was awarded the Victoria Cross for destroying an enemy machine-gun position and taking several prisoners near Poelcappelle, Belgium, on 12 October 1917 (see Appendix 4).

The artist and war poet Isaac Rosenberg, who was killed on 1 April 1918 near Fampoux. He had originally enlisted in the Suffolk Regiment, but later transferred to the 11th (Service) Battalion King's Own, a 'Bantam' Battalion raised in Lancaster in 1915. He served in D Company and went overseas with the Battalion in June 1916. On its disbandment in February 1918, he was transferred to the 1st Battalion. He is buried in Bailleul Road East Cemetery, St Laurent Blangy, France. *IWM Q101784*

Second Lieutenant Joseph Collin vc (posthumous), 1/4th Battalion (TF). He won the VC for outstanding bravery in holding his platoon position called 'Orchard Keep' and leading a fighting withdrawal until mortally wounded near Givenchy on 9 April 1918, during the German Spring Offensive (see Appendix 4).

A Lewis Gun No 2 of the 1/4th Battalion (TF), from a watercolour painted by Captain A. E. Ellwood MC in 1917 at Ypres. Albert Ellwood was killed in action at Givenchy on 14 April 1918.

Ellwood's grave in King's Liverpool Graveyard at Cuinchy; it was later moved to Vielle Chapelle Military Cemetery near Givenchy. The cross bears the enamel badge of the 55th West Lancashire Division (TF) and the motto 'THEY WIN OR DIE WHO WEAR THE ROSE OF LANCASTER'. These enamel badges were subscribed to by all ranks of the Division and one was attached to the cross of every 55th Division grave. The crosses were later replaced with headstones by the Imperial (later the Commonwealth) War Graves Commission.

Sergeant (later CSM) Victor Batty, DCM and bar, MM, Cross of the Russian Order of St George. Batty, of D Company 1st Battalion, photographed here wearing his DCM, Queen's S Africa Medal and Cross of St George, was killed near Bethune on 18 April 1918, when he was 'last seen fighting the Germans with his fists'.

Lance-Corporal James Hewitson VC, 1/4th Battalion (TF). He won his Victoria Cross for gallantry and leadership in clearing enemy-held trenches and dug-outs, and for attacking an enemy machine-gun position and bombing party single-handed, near Givenchy on 26 April 1918.

A quarter guard of the 1/5th Battalion (TF) at Bethune on 7 September 1918. *IWM Q9481*

Lance-Sergeant Tom Neely VC MM (posthumous), 8th (Service) Battalion. He was awarded the Victoria Cross for attacking several enemy strong-points and machine-gun positions in the Hindenburg Line near Flesquieres on 27 September 1918. Neely was killed in action four days later.

The 8th Battalion's Office, Cologne, Germany, 1919. *IWM Q3796*

Two men of the 2nd Battalion enjoying an ice from a street vendor in Chanak (Canakkale), Turkey, 1919, where they formed part of the occupying forces after the Armistice. *IWM Q14419*

Watched by the Mayor of Lancaster, Councillor William Briggs OBE, and the Corporation, the Cadre and Colours of the 1/5th Battalion (TF) parade in front of the Town Hall on their return from Germany via Ireland on 19 October 1919. The Commanding Officer, Lieutenant-Colonel W. G. Hoare DSO, stands to the left of the two mascots, Johnny, a white pony given by the 2nd Battalion, and Joey, an Indian mule found at Ypres in 1915. Captain H. B. Bennett MC carries the Regimental Colour and Captain W. N. Briggs the King's Colour. On the far left is the Quartermaster, Capt (Hon) A. H. Hodgkinson, who remained with the Battalion throughout the war and wrote a history of the unit published in 1921. As each Battalion of the Regiment was demobilised, the Cadre was met at Lancaster and given a civic reception by the Mayor and Corporation; the officers and men were entertained at the Town Hall. The 2/5th Battalion (TF), together with the five Service Battalions of the Regiment raised during the war which saw service abroad, received King's Colours, which were laid up in the Regimental Chapel at Lancaster Priory Church.

Chapter 7
1919-1939
THE ACTIVE PEACE

As the Cadres of the Service and Territorial Battalions returned home they were disbanded or stood down. The Cadre of the 1st Battalion went to Dublin in July 1919; it reformed the Battalion at Richmond Barracks, Inchicore, and was joined there by the Cadre and personnel of the 3rd (Special Reserve) Battalion and men from the 1/5th Battalion. The 1st Battalion remained in Ireland during the 'troubles' and carried out internal security duties until the formal truce was signed in late 1921 and a provisional government formed in January 1922. The Battalion was one of the last British Army units to leave Dublin, returning home to Shorncliffe in December 1922.

During the next few years the Battalion achieved great success on the sports field. Whilst at Aldershot the Rugby XV, captained by A. R. Aslett, won the Army Rugby Cup twice and the Aldershot Command Cup three times. In October 1930 the Battalion began an overseas tour, which took it to Haifa in Palestine. It was based at the Citadel Barracks, Cairo, from March 1932 until September 1934, when it moved to Wellington in Southern India. In September 1937 it moved to Madras.

The 2nd Battalion was re-formed at Tidworth in April 1919 and embarked for India and Burma in October. Companies and detachments were based at Bhamo, Mandalay and Maymyo. Sport again predominated, with successes in the Burma Cup and Calcutta competitions. The Battalion moved to Rawalpindi in north-west India in 1924 where, on 27 January 1926, it received New Colours, followed by a short posting in the Sudan from December 1929 until October 1930. In late December the Battalion sailed for England, arriving at Southampton on 7 January 1931. Based first at Lichfield and then at Aldershot from 1934, it continued the sporting success of the Regiment by winning the Army Football Cup in 1934 and by reaching the final of the Army Rugby Cup in 1936, when it lost to the Royal Tank Corps 11–0. In September 1938 the Battalion went to Palestine, where it carried out an anti-terrorist role, which included guarding the Sarafand–Jaffa–Jerusalem road, the railway through Gaza into Egypt, patrol work, searches for arms and explosives, and working parties. On 18 January 1939 one such group, commanded by Second Lieutenant Waring, was ambushed; Waring received the Military Cross and Sergeant Phenna the Military Medal for their actions during this engagement.

In 1920 the 4th and 5th Territorial Battalions were reformed, although it took some time before recruiting levels rose, while the Morecambe Company of the 5th Battalion was not reformed until the 1930s. Facilities, however, were improved with the building of new Drill Halls at Barrow (1928), Dalton (1929), Carnforth (1930), Millom

(1932) and Morecambe (1937). Mechanised transport was introduced in 1937. After Annual Camp in 1938 the 4th Battalion (TA) was converted into the 56th Anti-Tank Regiment (King's Own) RA TA and its officers and men transferred to the Royal Artillery. In May 1939, a duplicate unit, 66th Anti-Tank Regiment RA (King's Own) TA, was raised in Liverpool as part of the increase in the Territorial Army.

This period also included a number of events which further strengthened ties between the Regiment and the City of Lancaster. Seven stands of King's Own and Militia Colours were returned to the Regiment and laid up in the Chapel. In November 1924 Field Marshal Earl Haig unveiled the First World War Memorial and Shrine in the Regimental Chapel and formally opened the Westfield War Memorial Village, built for disabled ex-servicemen of the town. The Regiment's War Memorial in the Village was unveiled in 1926 and in December 1929 the Regimental Museum was opened in the Lancaster Museum.

In 1930 the Regiment celebrated its 250th Anniversary in Aldershot and also in Lancaster, where the 4th and 5th Battalions (TA) trooped their Regimental Colours on Giant Axe Field. In 1931 the Regimental Depot held its first 'At Home' day, when the general public could explore Bowerham Barracks; this was to become an annual event.

There were also a number of important developments for the Regimental family. The Regimental Association expanded after the First World War and several wartime Battalions formed their own reunion groups. The Regimental Magazine was revived in January 1921 and continued to publish a wealth of information. In 1931 the London Midland & Scottish Railway formally named 'Royal Scot' Class locomotive No 6161 *King's Own*. A Historical Committee was formed in 1933 with the aim of producing a Regimental history; subsequently the work of Colonels Grover, Keith and Cowper already referred to bore fruit in 1939 with the publication of the first two volumes of *The King's Own — The Story of a Royal Regiment*. In 1934 a Regimental Employment Committee was formed to assist former members of the Regiment in obtaining civilian employment on leaving the Army.

The first Old Comrades Association Dinner after the First World War, at the Royal King's Arms Hotel, Lancaster, on 6 August 1921. Many of those present have not yet received their medals, but wear the ribbons. Corporal James Hewitson VC of Coniston (see Appendix 4) sits on the front row (second from the right); the tunic he is wearing is now in the Regimental Museum.

The Band and Drums lead the 1st Battalion into the Royal Barracks for the Trooping of the Colour, St George's Day, Dublin, 1921. During the Battalion's 2½-year tour, there was only one fatality, Bandsman Mark Percival, who was killed in Dublin on 17 May 1921.

Colour Party of the 1st Battalion at Shorncliffe, St George's Day 1924. From the left: CSM Parrott, Lieutenant Brennand, CQMS Crane, Lieutenant Bazalgette and CSM Bill Bell MC. Bell is the only man in the Army to have been awarded the Military Cross as a Sergeant; he later became RSM and Quartermaster of the 1st Battalion and retired with the rank of Lieutenant-Colonel.

Field Marshal Earl Haig officially opens the Westfield War Memorial Village at Lancaster on 27 November 1924. He also unveiled the memorial shrine to men of the Regiment who died during the First World War in the Regimental Chapel on the same day. Westfield House and the land on which the village was built formed the estate of the late Sir Thomas Storey and was given by his family through his son Herbert L. Storey of Bailrigg, Lancaster. The village was designed by Thomas Mawson of Lancaster. Initially 35 cottages and bungalows were built by public and private subscription, with others added by 1930 and eight more in 1950. These provided houses for local men, mainly from the Regiment, who were disabled as a result of service during the First World War, and was a practical response to the effects of war, paralleled by only a few such projects in the United Kingdom. The foundation stone of the first cottage was laid by Lord Richard Cavendish CB CMG on 26 November 1919. Each house or bungalow bore a plate naming the group or individual benefactor who provided it: £500 paid for a cottage. Eventually each building bore the name of a famous battle or engagement, such as 'Ypres', 'Somme' and 'Le Cateau'.

General Sir Archibald Hunter, Colonel of the Regiment, officially unveils the War Memorial at Westfield Village on 4 August 1926. Also by the plinth are (from the left) Colonel G. Wilson, who lived at Westfield House and acted as Secretary of the Village Trust, Alderman Briggs, and Mr H. L. Storey. The memorial, depicting a soldier giving his wounded comrade a drink, was dedicated to all ranks of The King's Own Royal Regiment (Lancaster), the Lancaster Artillery Battery and other Lancastrians who had served during the war. The bronze figures were designed and modelled at the Storey Institute in Lancaster by Miss Delahunt.

The Officers of the 1st Battalion at Ramillies Barracks, Aldershot, on St George's Day 1927. Left to right, back row: 2/Lt Woolmer, Lt Fairfax-Lucy, Lt Howse, 2/Lt Daly, Lt Mears, Capt Seddon, Lt Head, Lt Gibson, Capt Beaumont, Edib Bey (Egyptian Army attached). Middle row: Capt Baker, Capt B. D. Armstrong, Capt Matthews (see p 75), Lt Wright, Lt Crow, 2/Lt Cooper with Regimental Colour, Capt White MC, Capt Somerville MC, Lt Carr MC DCM, Lt Johnson, Lt E. A. Carter. Front row: Maj J. F. B. Morrell DSO MVO, Col Gribbon CMG CBE, Lt and Adjt Aslett, Lt Col Kaulback, Col Nicholson CMG DSO, the Commanding Officer, Brig Gen O. C. Borrett, Brig Gen F. B. Matthews CB DSO, Maj Young DSO, Lt Col Johnson, Capt and Quartermaster A. W. Morrell MC, Lt Col Money. Note the rose in each individual's cap and the garland around the Regimental Colour. The Service Dress cap worn by officers had a leather edge to the peak, a uniform distinction which was probably unique to the Regiment.

A detachment of the 1st Battalion parades on the village green at Yately, Hampshire, with the 1799 King's Colour (on the right) restored to the Regiment in July 1927. It was given in 1816 to Colonel Faunce, who gave it in 1828 to Captain Mason; his daughter presented it in turn to Yately Parish Church in 1922. This was the first of several stands of old Colours to be returned to the Regiment and laid up in the Regimental Chapel at Lancaster.

The rugby and football teams of the 2nd Battalion, winners of the Burma Association Cup, Association Shield and the Burma Rugby Cup, at Maymyo, Burma, 1920.

The rugby team of the 1st Battalion, winners of the Army and Aldershot Command Cups in the 1928–29 season, Aldershot, 1929. This is the most famous and successful rugby team in the Regiment's history, winners of the Aldershot Command Cup in 1927, 1928 and 1929, finalists in the Army Cup in 1928 and winners in 1929 and 1930. Inset: Sgt W. Hall. Left to right, back row: Ptes Turner and Hopwood, Sgt Kenyon, Cpl Slocombe, Lt Haynes, Sgt Young, L/Cpl Richards, Sgt Hamblett. Front row: Pte Abbott, Sgt Morton, Capt Somerville MC, Lt A. R. Aslett (Captain), Lt Wright, Sgt J. Whelpton. On the ground: CQMS Cooney and L/Cpl Schofield. Morton and Whelpton both played for the Army, but the outstanding individual player was A. R. Aslett, who played 20 times for the Army and, as Captain of the side, achieved a record 11 victories out of 12. He played six times for England in 1926 and 1929, but injury prevented any further international appearances. Aslett commanded the 2nd Battalion and a Brigade in Burma during the Second World War, and was awarded the DSO and the American Legion of Honor.

Captain R. H. Horne TD speaks with HRH the Prince of Wales at Barrow-in-Furness on 29 July 1927. The 4th Battalion (TA) provided a Guard-of-Honour when the Prince visited the town.

Officers, NCOs, wives and children of the 2nd Battalion crowd the decks of HMT *Neuralia* as she leaves Bombay for Sudan on 5 December 1929. The *Neuralia* was a familiar transport to The King's Own and took the 2nd Battalion home to England in 1931.

On the promenade deck facing the camera are, from right to left: Mrs Briggs's nurse, Maj Carter, Mrs Green, Capt Briggs, Capt Hardy, Mrs Briggs, Mrs Connell, Mrs Hardy, Mrs Bevan, Maj Connell, Maj Morrell, children, unknown, Sgt Evans, Lt Tilly, RSM Brooks, unknown, Lt Creedon, Lt Carter. On the lower deck, from left to right: Sgt Kilbride, Mrs Kilbride, CSM Harper, CSM Bowles, Sgt McCabe. The Commanding Officer, Lieutenant-Colonel (Brevet Colonel) W. H. Gribbon CMG CBE, stands on the gangway. Colonel Gribbon commanded the Battalion in Rawalpindi, Khartoum and Lichfield.

Soldiers of the 2nd Battalion disembark from HMT *Neuralia* at Southampton on 7 January 1931. The Battalion returned home after 18 years service abroad.

Lord Derby gives his address at the official opening of the Regimental Museum in Lancaster Museum on 10 December 1929. Looking on are the Mayor, Councillor T. Till, members of the Corporation and Regimental guests including Major L. I. Cowper OBE, then commanding the Regimental Depot. The Regimental Museum was the first to be established on municipal premises, something which is now quite common since the amalgamation of regiments and the closure of regimental depots. The Museum was closed at the outbreak of the Second World War and the collections placed in store until July 1946; the Canadian Forces Treasury occupied the building during the war. Lancaster City Council (Borough Council until 1937) maintains the Museum, which is just one example of the close links between the Regiment and the City which have continued since 1959 with its successor The King's Own Royal Border Regiment.

A wheelbarrow race during the celebration of the Regiment's 250th Anniversary. 1st Battalion, Aldershot, July 1930.

The London Midland & Scottish Railway 'Royal Scot' Class locomotive No 6161 *King's Own*, built at Derby Works in 1930 and originally named *The King's Own*. It was renamed by Brigadier-General F. B. Matthews CB DSO, Deputy Colonel of the Regiment, at Euston Station on 7 January 1931. The 2nd Battalion, which disembarked the same day at Southampton, travelled to London to witness the ceremony. As its first public duty after naming, the locomotive hauled the train conveying the Battalion to Lichfield. The locomotive was rebuilt in 1949 and eventually withdrawn in 1963. British Railways presented the Regiment with one of the nameplates, which is now in the Regimental Museum.

The Colours of Barrell's Regiment (A) and the Colour of the Stewarts of Appin (B) carried at the Battle of Culloden on 16 April 1746, together with the Regimental Colours of the 2nd Battalion King's Own Royal Regiment (C), the Colour of the Atholl Highlanders (D) and their representative detachments, in front of the Scottish War Memorial at Edinburgh Castle on 1 August 1931. Lieutenant R. W. Hallam carries the King's Colour of Barrells, Lieutenant W. V. H. Robins the Regimental Colour, and Lieutenant B. A. Burke the 2nd Battalion's Regimental Colour. The Appin Colour is one of the few Jacobite Colours to survive from Culloden, as most were burned by the public hangman in Edinburgh after the Battle. It was brought back to Stewart of Ballachulish, with whose family it remained. Barrell's Colours were replaced probably in 1751, and were acquired *circa* 1830 by General Stewart of Garth, who gave them to Stewart of Ballachulish 'so that the flags which were opposed to each other at Culloden might hereafter rest in peace, side by side'. The Stewart Society acquired the three Colours and, according to the wishes of the Stewarts of Ballachulish, arranged for them to be deposited in the Scottish National Naval and Military Museum (now the Scottish United Services Museum) in Edinburgh Castle on 31 August 1931, where they remain.

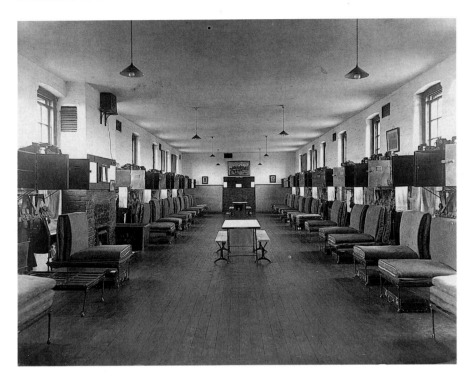

Soldiers' barrack-room, Bowerham Barracks, Lancaster, *circa* 1933. Compare this with the 1897 view on p43 and the 1951 view on p158.

Kit laid out for inspection, weekly (left) and daily (right), 2nd Battalion, Lichfield, *circa* 1933 — compare this with 1902 (p61). A former recruit at the Regimental Depot in 1936 recalls being issued with these photographs to show him how to lay his kit out.

The football team of the 2nd Battalion which won the Army Cup in 1934, beating the 2nd Battalion Royal Tank Corps 3–0 on 2 April at the Command Central Ground, Aldershot, before a crowd of 8–10,000. Left to right, back row: Sergeant A. White (trainer), Lieutenant W. W. Bell MC (i/c football), Lance-Corporal Stan Eastham, Dmr Charlie Brown, Bandsman Harry Sowerbutts, Bandsman Harry Bonehill, Lance-Corporal Albert Lyness, Private Maurice Vickers, CSM Freddie Parker (team manager). Front row: Lance-Corporal W. E. Brown (Winny), CSM J. Wilcox (Stiffy), Lieutenant-Colonel J. Bois DSO MC, Lieutenant W. V. H. Robins (Captain), Lance-Sergeant Benny Lowe, Corporal G. Cannon Hughes. The King's Own became one of the few Regiments to win both the Army Rugby and Football cups. Of the team Robins, Sowerbutts, Eastham, Lyness, Vickers and Bonehill played for the Army, while Eastham also played as an Amateur International for England and Lyness for Ireland. Robins captained the Army Team and took a Combined Services Team, which included Eastham, to South Africa in 1936. Eastham also represented England in the touring team to New Zealand and Australia in 1937 and at the Berlin Olympic Games in 1936.

Private J. Gillibrand, 1st Battalion, Cairo, 1933. One of the most famous boxers in the Regiment, he was Heavyweight Champion Middle East and Amateur Light Heavyweight Champion of Egypt in 1933.

Lance Corporal Alf Bastow, clutching the winner's rosette between his teeth, leads the 2nd Battalion's winning team in the Driving Cup Competition on a lap of honour, at the 1934 Catterick Command Horse Show. Bastow, an ex-rough rider, was the Battalion farrier and Heavyweight Boxing Champion and was known as 'one-shot Bastoe' due to his ability to fell opponents regularly with a single punch. The other member of the team is Private Nobby Hall, and the horses Minnie, Herbert, Betty and Bert.

The drums of the 5th Battalion (TA) following refurbishment and re-emblazoning by Messrs Boosey and Hawkes Limited in 1935. The Mayoress of Lancaster, Mrs Simpson, and Lady Ashton established a Band and Drums fund, which raised £500 towards this work and the provision of new instruments. Lady Ashton also presented the Battalion with a new Drum-Major's sash.

The 2nd Battalion, led by Brigadier-General Sir T. D. Jackson DSO MVO, the Deputy Colonel of the Regiment, marches past HM King George V during the Silver Jubilee Royal Review at the Rushmoor Arena, Aldershot, in July 1935.

The Sikh Platoon of the 1st Battalion, Wellington Barracks, southern India, 1935. Each infantry Battalion in India was allotted one such platoon on the abolition of the Machine Gun Corps to provide additional machine-gun support. Many of the platoon wear Indian General Service medals with several bars. The King's Own cap-badge was worn on the left of the turban, on a blue background with an orange/gold fringe. The 1st Battalion's Sikh Platoon was formed in 1934 and disbanded in 1938.

The King's Birthday Garrison Parade at Wellington Barracks on 9 June 1937. No 1 and No 2 Companies with Colour Party are from the 1st Battalion King's Own, and the other five Companies are from the 1st Battalions of the West Yorkshire, Gloucestershire and North Staffordshire Regiments. The massed bands of The King's Own and Gloucestershire Regiments are directed by Bandmaster W. J. Gibbs, Gloucestershire Regiment (late King's Own). Wellington was the home of the 1st Battalion from September 1934 to September 1937.

The Mayor of Lancaster, Councillor J. G. E. Clark, visits the Quartermaster's stores during a tour of the 5th Battalion's Drill Hall at Phoenix Street, Lancaster, on 20 February 1936, as a new recruit receives his kit from the Quartermaster, Lieutenant E. Williams DCM, watched by RQMS Marsden. Lieutenant Williams was the son of QM Sergeant Ellis Williams (1850–1922), who served in the Regiment and published a book of poetry, *Ballads of the King's Own*. He also ran the post office in Bowerham Road, a short distance from the barracks, which his son Lieutenant Williams took over and his son after him: all three were named Ellis. During the First World War, six Williams brothers served in the Army, four of them, including Ellis, in The King's Own.

The procession party from the 2nd Battalion for the Coronation of HM King George VI in 1937. Left to right: Major R. H. Welch DSO, RSM Ralph, CSM Baxter, CQMS Atkinson, Sergeant Richmond, Corporal Worsley, Lance-Corporal Waters and Private Evans, all of whom received the Coronation Medal.

Groups from the Regimental Depot, dressed in the uniforms of 1680, 1742, 1815 and the (then) present day, march down Cheapside in the procession to celebrate the conferring of City status on Lancaster by King George VI in 1937.

Drum-Major Tyler, with the Band and Drums, leads the 2nd Battalion down from Windsor Castle after the restoration of the 1859 Colours to the Regiment by the Earl of Athlone, Constable of the Castle, on behalf of King George VI on 9 July 1937. Lieutenant E. W. Matthews received the Queen's Colour and Lieutenant N. St G. Gribbon the Regimental Colour. These Colours had been laid up in the chapel at Windsor following the presentation of new Colours to the 2nd Battalion by Queen Victoria on 6 December 1878 (see p39). They were laid up in the Regimental Chapel at Lancaster on 28 November 1937.

The mechanised transport of the 2nd Battalion, Aldershot, 1937. The transport consists of eight BSA motorcycles, seven Austin 7 cars, 20 Morris-Commercial CS8 15 cwt trucks, six Morris-Commercial 30 cwt trucks and one Morris-Commercial CS8 Water-bowser.

Soldiers of the 2nd Battalion give a demonstration of kapok bridging for King George VI at Minley Manor Lake, Aldershot, 1938.

The Colonel of the Regiment, Lieutenant-General O. C. Borrett KCB CMG CBE DSO, **accompanied by Lieutenant-Colonel N. M. Ritchie** DSO MC, **the Commanding Officer, inspects the 2nd Battalion at Blenheim Barracks, Aldershot, prior to its departure for Palestine, September 1938.**

A Lewis-gun team of the 1st Battalion practising during a passive air-raid scheme, Madras, southern India, 12 October 1938.

2nd Battalion platoon post at Al-Walaja on the Jerusalem to Jaffa railway line, Palestine, 1939. All ranks who had served in Palestine up to 3 September 1939 received the General Service Medal with clasp 'PALESTINE'.

A 2nd Battalion motorised trolley preceding a Palestine Railways train on the Gaza to Jaffa railway line, Palestine, 1938–39. The trolley was used to detect mines or explosives on the line, which was regularly sabotaged.

Men of the 2nd Battalion searching Arab villagers for weapons and explosives, Palestine, 1939.

A 2nd Battalion Morris-Commercial 15 cwt truck loaded with one section, Palestine, 1938–39. The Battalion formed a motorised company for patrol work, each truck being fitted with steel plates on the floors and a layer of sandbags as protection against land-mines. Sufficient rations, water and ammunition were carried for each section. The soldiers wear khaki overalls, known as 'Goonskins', which were made up by the Regiment's Indian tailor and provided additional protection during patrol work over rough terrain.

Chelsea Pensioners and Boy Soldiers of the 2nd Battalion at Aldershot on St George's Day 1938. Left to right, back row: Boys R. Baines, W. Miskelly, F. Bradford and T. Hunt. Front row: In-Pensioners H. R. Russell, H. Lee, J. Gray and W. Collis. The Boy Soldiers, since they were under age, had to remain in the UK when the Battalion went to Palestine, but Tommy Hunt eventually joined his Battalion in Ceylon in 1942 as it prepared to begin jungle warfare training.

The carrier platoon of the 5th Battalion (TA) at Summer Camp, Abergavenny, South Wales, August 1939.

Militiamen arriving at Bowerham Barracks in July 1939. The passing of the Military Training Act in May of that year required all men to register for two years' compulsory service. These 'Militiamen' were to complete six months full-time service, before transferring to the Territorials for the rest of their engagement. The first Militiamen arrived at Bowerham Barracks on 15 July, and were accommodated in new wooden barracks built on the barrack field between Bowerham Road and the Main Gate. Those Militiamen who completed sufficient service qualified for the Territorial Efficiency Medal bar MILITIA, in addition to any other service medals granted for war service.

Sons of the Regiment serving with the 1st Battalion, at Napier Barracks, Karachi, December 1939. Left to right, back row: Bdsm Taylor, Bdsm Patton, Sgt Drennan, Bdsm Eyre, L/Cpl Worsley, Pte Dixon, Cpl Hornby, Pte Parrington, Pte Hollis, Pte Blamire. Front row: Sgt Murphy, PSM Curtis, 2/Lt H. P. Burke, Capt J. H. M. Young, 2/Lt N. St G. Gribbon, 2/Lt R. L. J. Pott, Sgt Cronshaw.

Chapter 8
1939-1945
ACTIONS ON THREE CONTINENTS

The Regiment's role during the Second World War was very different from that of 1914–18. Its Battalions travelled further, were in action in more countries, spent much longer training and less time in the front line and, in some cases, gave up their infantry role altogether. The Regiment had fewer Battalions and suffered fewer casualties. Moreover, although it still drew a high percentage of its manpower from the Regimental area and Lancashire as a whole, its soldiers came from all over the country.

At the outbreak of war the 1st Battalion, stationed at Napier Barracks in Karachi, was carrying out security duties on the coast and at Karachi Docks. The 2nd Battalion remained in Palestine. In Lancaster, the Infantry Training Centre at Bowerham Barracks and the Camp at Middleton were full of both Militiamen and wartime conscripts.

The 5th Battalion (TA) and 56th Anti-Tank Regiment RA (King's Own) TA were mobilised in September as part of 42nd (East Lancashire) Division (TA), which in April 1940 joined the British Expeditionary Force (BEF) in France. In February 1940 four King's Own Pioneer Battalions, the 6th, 7th, 8th and 9th, were formed with the role of carrying out construction work, mainly the building of defences for units of the BEF, although they were still expected to carry out normal infantry duties when required. The personnel for these Battalions came from all over the country and from almost every Regiment and unit in the Army. They also joined the BEF in April.

Following the German invasion on 10 May, these Battalions made their way back to Dunkirk, lacking in many cases basic infantry equipment, including carriers and bren-guns. There was also the constant threat of air attack and the problems created by roads blocked with refugees. The 6th Battalion fought a determined rearguard action at Merville, while the 5th Battalion and 56 Anti-Tank Regiment provided the defence on a section of the Dunkirk perimeter before being evacuated.

On their return to England, the Territorials and Pioneers were employed on anti-invasion duties and coastal defence. Several experienced a change of role. The 5th Battalion, together with the 10th Battalion, which had been formed in the autumn of 1940, were converted to armour in January 1942 as 107th Regiment RAC (King's Own) and 151st Regiment RAC. In December 1943 107th was disbanded and its personnel transferred to 151st, which assumed 107th's title in January 1944. The Regiment, although Royal Armoured Corps, was badged King's Own.

56th and 66th Anti-Tank Regiments both lost batteries, which were used to form other units; 223 Battery from 56th became 1st Air-Landing Anti-

Tank Battery in November 1941 and served with the 1st Airborne Division on Sicily in 1943 and at Arnhem in 1944. 56th Anti-Tank Regiment went out to India in 1941 and fought in India and Burma from October 1943 until the end of the war, while 66th Anti-Tank Regiment remained in the UK throughout the war. The 6th Battalion also remained in the UK until disbandment in July 1944. The 7th Battalion, however, went to Gibraltar in June 1942 and, after a brief period in the UK, left for India in March 1943, where it remained until after the war. After intensive training, it was a great disappointment for many in the Battalion not to see active service. The 9th Battalion remained in the UK and was converted to artillery in 1941.

The 8th Battalion left Scotland for Malta in July 1941. *En route,* on 23 July, HMS *Manchester,* carrying the majority of the Battalion, was torpedoed and had to limp back to Gibraltar. The Battalion finally arrived in Malta on board other ships on 2 August, and remained on the island until November 1943, during the period of the siege, its main role being to provide the defence for various airfields; Battalion headquarters were at Ta Salvatur. The Battalion became extremely proficient in building stone U-shaped pens on the airfield to protect the aircraft from being 'spitchered' (from the Maltese *spiccha* — to break) or burned out. It also provided working parties to help unload the ships that arrived with supplies.

On arrival in Palestine, the Battalion was able to carry out some proper infantry training. With the virtual destruction of the 1st Battalion on Leros, one of the Dodecanese Islands off the Turkish coast, in November 1943, the 8th Battalion absorbed the details and the few men (one officer and 57 other ranks) who escaped from Leros, assumed the title of the 1st Battalion on 30 January 1944, and joined the 10th (Indian) Division.

The original 1st Battalion remained in Karachi until April 1941, when 350 officers and other ranks were airlifted to the RAF station at Shaibah, near Basra in Iraq. This followed a coup d'état by the pro-German Iraqi Prime Minister Raschid Ali, who declared war on Britain on 28 April. Through a Treaty of 1930 the British held several airfields in Iraq, and had secured access for her forces through the country. On 27 April the Battalion was airlifted to RAF Habbaniya to the west of Baghdad and provided the ground defence of the airfield.

In early May the Battalion, with a company of Iraqi Levies and aircraft from the RAF Flying Training School, attacked and overran enemy forces threatening the plateau overlooking the airfield. Between 19 and 22 May, supported by Gurkhas and Iraqi Levies, it moved east to defeat an Iraqi counter-attack at Fallujah, thus opening the way to Baghdad. For this the Regiment received the unique Battle Honour 'Defence of Habbaniya'. The Battalion then moved into northern Iraq to secure the airfield at Mosul for the RAF; it was based at various locations including Kirkuk, Ramadi and Haffa with other units of 25th Indian Infantry Brigade as occupying forces. Its duties included guarding oil pipelines and pumping stations. The 1st Battalion remained in Iraq until a move to the Western Desert in May 1942.

In early June 1942 the Battalion was in a defensive position known as the Sollum Box on the Libyan-Egyptian frontier. After the fall of Tobruk, the Battalion withdrew to Mersa Matruh, then on 29 June it was ordered to break out towards Fuka airfield and El Alamein. A large number of the Battalion were killed, wounded or captured during the withdrawal. The remainder left Port Said for Cyprus on 17 August aboard the *Princess Marguerite,* which was torpedoed *en route*; one officer and 23 other ranks were lost. Private Crellin was awarded the British Empire Medal for saving the lives of a number of men.

The Battalion was reformed on Cyprus with men from the 1st Battalions of the South Wales Borderers and Duke of Cornwall's Light Infantry. After training in Syria and Palestine in 1943, the Battalion was sent to Leros on 5 November. Deprived of air cover, The King's Own and three other British Infantry Battalions were subject to a German airborne and sea landing on 12 November. After fierce fighting the island surrendered on the 16th; the 1st Battalion lost 54 killed, including 15 officers, and an unknown number of wounded and prisoners-of-war.

After amalgamation, the new 1st Battalion landed in Italy on 28 March 1944, and following a period of training and service in the line on the Adriatic Front it moved with 10th Indian Division to the Tiber Valley on 26 June. After the capture of Umbertide, the Battalion carried out a superb flank attack on the village of Montone on 7 July, followed by a night attack on 16 July, which opened the road to Citta di Castello. In October the Battalion fought in the Adriatic sector, taking San Martino, followed by the heavy fighting to secure and retain Pideura Ridge west of Faenza in December 1944. The Battalion was on the River Senio in January 1945 and later at Monte Grande until April 1945; it was resting at Ferrara in northern Italy when the campaign ended on 2 May.

The 2nd Battalion arrived at Helwan in Egypt from Palestine in June 1940, and from August to December it was based in defensive positions around Mersa Matruh in the Western Desert. After returning to Egypt it fought in two actions against Vichy French forces in Syria, near Merjayoun in late June 1941 and on the mountainous Jebel Mazar in July. A DSO, an MC and five MMs were awarded for these actions. In September the Battalion arrived by sea in Tobruk as part of the British 6th Division to replace the Australians. The King's Own was based on the perimeter defences and the monotonous routine was accompanied only by regular enemy fire and poor rations. On 21 November 1941 the Battalion successfully attacked enemy strong points known as 'Butch' and 'Jill' on the south-east corner of the perimeter in an operation referred to as the 'Tobruk Sortie'.

The Battalion left Tobruk for Egypt on 21 December and in March 1942 moved to Ceylon and later India, where it carried out extensive jungle training. From March until July 1944, as No 41 and 46 Chindit Columns, the Battalion operated behind the lines in northern Burma, where the arduous conditions were just as much the enemy as the Japanese. In late May 1944 both Columns were involved in an extremely fierce action inside 'Blackpool Block', a defensive perimeter south-west of Myitkyina. In June, despite losses through casualties and disease, the Battalion assisted in operations against Mogaung, and in July the survivors were taken by jeep to Myitkyina and flown to India, having marched over 1,100 miles during the Campaign.

In July 1944 107th Regiment RAC (King's Own) landed in Normandy as part of 34th Independent Armoured Brigade and fought in support of various infantry divisions during the campaign in North West Europe. 107th saw action at Hill 112 near Esquay, south-west of Caen, in July, followed by various actions to the south of Caen in August, including heavy fighting at Grimbosq and Brieux in the Orne Bridgehead on the 7th and 8th. In September 1944 107th supported 49th (West Riding) Division in the capture of Le Havre and in October fought several engagements from Loenhout and Wuestwezel in northern Belgium up to Wouw in south-west Holland. It supported 15th (Scottish) Division in the capture of Blerick in December, and in the following February fought its final actions of the war with 51st (Highland) Division in the Reichswald Forest, on the Dutch-German border. The Regiment crossed the Rhine on 7 April 1945 and was based near Munster on VE Day.

The other units affiliated to the Regiment during the war were the Home Guard. Four Battalions covering Barrow-in-Furness, North Lonsdale, Lancaster and South Lonsdale were badged King's Own and included many former members of the Regiment.

During the Second World War the Regiment suffered 869 officers and other ranks killed or died of wounds. The Regiment was awarded 20 Battle Honours and the Honorary Distinction NORTH-WEST EUROPE, granted to the 5th Battalion (TA), which had originally formed 107th Regiment RAC. This total is far fewer than for the First World War, but it should be noted that, as armoured and artillery units, 107th Regiment RAC and 56th Anti-Tank Regiment did not qualify for Battle Honours.

B Company 5th Battalion (TA) after mobilisation, photographed outside the Drill Hall, Preston Street, Fleetwood, in September 1939.

Far from home, Santa Claus and the Christmas tree arrive watched by children from the 1st Battalion, Karachi, India, December 1939.

Headquarters personnel of 56th Anti-Tank Regiment (King's Own) RA TA, prior to leaving for France in April 1940. Left to right, front row: RSM Brierley, Lt E. Braithwaite (RAMC), Maj T. Toler, Lt Col Palmer TD, Maj J. Thompson, 2/Lt P. Wood, Lt Hannigan, RQMS Morrison.

Officers of the 7th Battalion at Colchester, 19 April 1940, prior to leaving for France.

Troops from the Depot at the 'Soldier's Club' in the Baptist Schoolroom, Robert Street, Lancaster, 1940. The club, opened by Lady Ashton on 1 October 1939, was open in the evenings from 6–10 pm and on Saturdays and Sundays from 2.30 pm. It provided somewhere for soldiers to spend their leisure hours and had a lounge with newspapers, magazines and writing materials, a lending library, a games/club room and a canteen. One former serviceman recalls that meat and potato pie with beans cost 3d.

The Royal Visit to the Regimental Depot and King's Own Infantry Training Centre, Bowerham Barracks, Lancaster, 2 May 1940. The King, accompanied by Lieutenant-Colonel R. P. F. White MC (on the left), the Depot Commander, speaks with Sergeant H. G. 'Tich' Phenna MM after visiting the miniature range. Sergeant Phenna won his MM in Palestine, whilst serving with the 2nd Battalion in January 1939.

During the same visit Queen Elizabeth inspects the ATS contingent, accompanied by Commandant Mrs Barton. Captain J. Aylmer-Hall, the Orderly Officer, and Lady Halifax, Lady-in-Waiting, follow behind. On 10 September 1939 the Regiment Depot was re-designated the King's Own Infantry Training Centre (ITC), and soldiers received their 16 weeks basic training here before being posted to their Battalion. To accommodate the large number of extra troops, Middleton Tower Holiday Camp, near Heysham, and Heysham Towers Holiday Camp were taken over by the Army. In August 1941 the King's Own ITC closed and training was transferred to No 18 ITC at Hadrian's Camp, Carlisle, which included a King's Own Training Company. For the remainder of the war the Barracks were occupied by a small Regimental Depot party, No 4 ATS Depot and later a Battalion of the Border Regiment.

Soldiers from the King's Own Infantry Training Centre at a display during Birmingham War Weapons Week, 1940. War Weapons Week was organised throughout the country to raise money for the war effort.

Soldiers of the 6th Battalion training with a Boyes anti-tank rifle, probably at Castle Howard, North Yorkshire, in 1940. *IWM H4577*

The cook-house detail, 2nd Battalion, Helwan, Egypt, 1940. From left to right: Privates Muir, McGuiness, Salmon and Lovatt, Sergeant Farrington and Privates Hailwood, Rayson, Mills and Tombling. The Battalion arrived at Helwan on the River Nile above Cairo on 10 June and was responsible for the defence of the nearby aerodrome. It moved to the barracks at Abassia near Cairo on 6 August. *IWM E238*

Officers of the 2nd Battalion at Helwan in June 1940. Left to right, back row: Rev Winstanley (Padre), Capt Bazalgette, 2/Lt Darlington, 2/Lt Harris, Lt Jebb, Lt Wickham, 2/Lt Robinson, Lt Bellamy, Capt Jordan (RAMC), 2/Lt McLeish, Lt Waring MC, 2/Lt Evans, Lt O'Sullivan. Middle row, sitting: Maj Howse, Maj Fitzsimon MC, Capt Hallam, Maj Creedon. Front row: Capt Leigh, Capt (QM) Parkinson, Lt Lincoln, 2/Lt Batchelor. *IWM E246*

Soldiers of the 2nd Battalion preparing anti-tank mines near Mersa Matruh, Egypt, October 1940. From mid-August the Battalion formed part of the garrison of the fortress, which it defended under air attack from the Luftwaffe and the Italian Air Force and against the threatened invasion of Egypt by Italian ground forces, which had reached Sidi Barrani in mid-September. In December the MT section and Carrier Platoon were involved in the advance along the coast, whilst the remainder of the Battalion held Matruh and prepared POW cages for the thousands of Italian prisoners. *IWM E943*

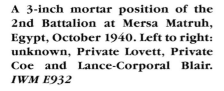

A 3-inch mortar position of the 2nd Battalion at Mersa Matruh, Egypt, October 1940. Left to right: unknown, Private Lovett, Private Coe and Lance-Corporal Blair. *IWM E932*

The Warrant Officers and Sergeants of the 5th Battalion (TA) in Suffolk, Christmas 1940. Left to right, back row: Sgts Reed, Beavers, Parker, Barwick, Farrell, Ford, Gardner. Fourth row: Sgts Mawson, J. Roberts, Lavelle, Gibson, Rawcliffe DCM, Stephens, Jenkins, Dormand, Greer, Hart. Third row: Sgts Gillibrand, Underwood, Wade, O'Malley, Woods, Alberts, Whittle, Tague, Gainer, Greene, Younger, Gates, Revill. Second row: Sgts Myers, Wilkinson and Watson, CQM Sgts Leadbetter, Cavanagh and Watson, PSMs Howson and Ball, CQM Sgts Gosling, Tymon and McKernan, Sgts Miller and Knight. Front row, sitting: CSMs King, Northam and Wright, OR Sgt McFetridge, Capt and Adjt Richardson MC, Lt Col Goldie OBE, RSM Heaysman, Maj Head, RQMS Kenyon, Lt and QM Lucas, CSMs Berry, W. Roberts and Hornby.

A soldier of the 1st Battalion with Iraqi prisoners at the RAF station at Habbaniya, west of Baghdad, Iraq, May 1941. The 1st Battalion was flown from Karachi to Iraq in April 1941 to provide the defence of RAF Treaty Airfields, following a German-inspired coup d'état. This was the first strategical air move by a major British unit. The Battalion participated in the defence of RAF Habbaniya then, on 6 May, whilst the RAF dealt with the Iraqi Air Force, the Battalion, supported by Iraqi levies and RAF armoured cars, cleared Iraqi ground forces from around the airfield. Captain Pat Weir was awarded the MC and Private J. McDermott the MM for gallantry during the action. Two Iraqi officers and 409 other ranks were taken prisoner. *IWM CM815*

Major W. V. H. Robins (centre) and another officer meeting with a Russian officer on the northern border of Persia in September 1941; British troops (8th Indian Division) had occupied the country in August 1941 to deter any German incursions. On 4 September Major Robins, with two other officers, the Medical Officer and a platoon of B Company, 1st Battalion, then stationed at Mosul in northern Iraq, went up to meet the Russians. The party returned to Mosul on 10 September. *IWM RR146*

Officers of the 2nd Battalion outside their Headquarters at Tobruk, October 1941. Left to right: Major H. E. ('Cracker') Creedon, Lieutenant-Colonel J. A. ('Jockey') Barraclough DSO OBE MC, and Captains Les Heap and Jack Slade. Barraclough, who had won his MC in the First World War, had been awarded the DSO for the Battalion's successful operations in Syria against the Vichy French in July. Les Heap and Jack Slade were both commissioned from the ranks; the former was one of the few officers to serve throughout the war with the Battalion, finally as a Column Commander in Burma during the Chindit operations. Creedon took over command of the Battalion in late October 1941 when Colonel Barraclough was evacuated sick. *IWM E6433*

A 2nd Battalion Vickers machine-gun position on the perimeter defences at Tobruk, November 1941. *IWM E6444*

Private F. Chadwick from Preston in his cook-house sited in a former Italian anti-tank ditch. 2nd Battalion, Tobruk, late 1941. *IWM E6443*

Major Sam Waring MC and bar and Corporal Arthur Milloy MM of Manchester with a captured Italian Breda machine-gun in one of the 2nd Battalion's outposts at Tobruk in November 1941. Major Waring won his Military Cross in Palestine in January 1939 and received a bar for his leadership of B Company during an attack on Vichy French positions at Jebel Mazar, Syria, on 10 July 1941. Corporal Milloy won his Military Medal for gallantry in leading a section of B Company in the same action. Waring, according to many who knew him, was destined to command a Battalion and was greatly respected for his calmness under fire. However, wounded on 24 November, he was evacuated but died at sea on 5 December 1941 when the hospital ship he was on was torpedoed. *IWM E6451*

Men of the 2nd Battalion don their overalls and desert boots as they prepare to go on patrol near Tobruk in late 1941. *IWM E6455*

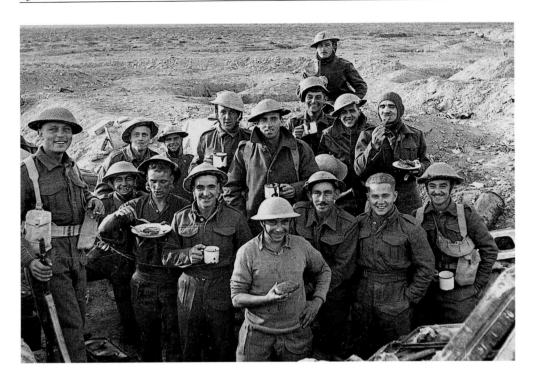

A group of the 2nd Battalion in a captured enemy position at El Acroma, south-west of Tobruk, December 1941. *IWM E7066*

Soldiers of the 2nd Battalion mount AA guard in the fort at El Acroma in December 1941. The fort and other positions had been captured by the 4th Indian Division on 11 December, and were occupied by the Battalion until it returned to Tobruk on 16 December. *IWM E7114*

The cruiser HMS *Manchester* which was attacked by Italian torpedo-bombers *en route* from Gibraltar to Malta with soldiers of the 8th Battalion on board on 23 July 1941. The ship developed a heavy list to port, and the soldiers assisted the crew in moving stores and equipment to the starboard side which helped to partially right the list. The ship, although badly damaged, managed to limp back to Gibraltar; a number of the crew and five officers and seven men of the Battalion were killed. The Battalion resumed its journey to Malta on the cruisers HMS *Hermione* and *Arethusa* and the minelayer HMS *Manxman* on 1 August, arriving at the Grand Harbour, Valetta, the following day. During the voyage HMS *Hermione* rammed and sank an Italian submarine.

Officers of the 8th Battalion, Malta, late 1941. Left to right, back row: Lt Sharpe, 2/Lt Grimes, Capt Mills, Lt Thornton, 2/Lt Chater, Capt Rhodes, 2/Lt Ratcliffe, 2/Lt Johnson, Lt Beesley, Lt Keith-Robinson. Middle row: Capt MacDonald, 2/Lt Freeman, Lt Turner, Lt Stephenson, Lt Brigden, 2/Lt Drewery, 2/Lt Dull-ender, Capt Griffiths (MO), Lt Brady, Capt Warren, Lt Davenport. Front row: Capt Stewart, Maj Morrison, Maj Stanton, Lt Coates (QM), Capt Clemence (Adjt), Lt-Col Westropp (CO), Maj Davidson (2I/C), Maj Hunt-ington, Capt Garnett, Capt Martin. Absent: Lt Booker.

Signallers of the 8th Battalion at Ta Salvatur, Malta, 1942. Note the 'stone wall' camouflage on the helmets and the bicycles, which were used extensively owing to the lack of petrol during the siege.

Quartermaster Sergeant Joe Rothblatt with the ration cart of HQ Company, 8th Battalion, near Hompesch, Malta, 1942.

Sergeants Lawford and Brown, 8th Battalion, writing home, Gomerino, Malta, 1943. Whilst on Malta the Battalion wore the shoulder title 'THE KING'S OWN' on the battledress blouse instead of the usual 'KING'S OWN'.

Major W. T. P. Tilly with C Company, 1st Battalion, Syria, 1943. The Battalion was virtually wiped out in November 1943 whilst defending the island of Leros in the Dodecanese. Fifty-four officers and other ranks were killed, and an unknown number wounded and taken prisoner. Eventually one officer and 57 other ranks returned to Palestine.

Men of the South Lonsdale Battalion Home Guard with a Browning .3 inch machine-gun during a weapons demonstration on the promenade adjacent to the Midland Hotel at Morecambe.

Men of the Machine Gun Platoon of the Lancaster City Battalion Home Guard are inspected by Major-General Johnson VC at Crag Bank Camp near Carnforth, 13 June 1943. Four Home Guard Battalions were badged King's Own — Barrow, North Lonsdale, Lancaster City and South Lonsdale — and each wore the shoulder flash EL (East Lancashire) with the Battalion number 1, 2, 3 or 4.

At the other extreme of wartime experience, Private Rostance (Commando) and Corporal Joe Cush, 1st Battalion, enjoy some hot food courtesy of the Royal Fusiliers on reaching Allied lines after their escape from POW camp, Italy, 1943. Corporal Cush was taken prisoner during the withdrawal from Mersa Matruh to El Alamein in June 1942. *IWM NA9874*

Officers of the 2nd Battalion at Imphal, India, prior to the Chindit operations, 1944. Left to right, back row: Capt P. Edwards RA, Lt Dodd, Lt Stock, Lt Hart, Lt Leyland, Capt Brown RAMC (MO 46 COL), Lt Coleman, Capt Openshaw, Capt G. Edwards, Capt Busby, Rev Rae (Padre 46 COL), Flt-Lt Robinson RAF (41 COL), Capt Pike, Lt Horne, Rev Miller (Padre 41 COL), Flt-Lt Rhodes (46 COL). Middle row: Capt Tucker, Capt Winmill, Maj Royle, Maj Heap (CO 46 COL), Lt-Col A. W. Thompson MC (CO 41 COL), Maj Robinson, Maj Rees, Capt Gibb RAMC (MO 41 COL), Capt Kershaw RA, Capt Brown. Front row: unknown, Lt Harrison, Lt Green RA, Lt Shaw, Lt Betts RE, Lt Littlewood, Lt Oliver RE, Lt Jordan, Lt Morris.

The stores and supplies for 41 and 46 Columns, 2nd Battalion, ready for loading at Imphal, India, March 1944. Both Columns were flown from Imphal to the airstrip at 'Broadway', south-west of Myitkyina, northern Burma, on 9 March.

Major Les Heap, CO of No 46 Column 2nd Battalion, taking a bath in Burma in April 1944. Major Heap, who commanded 46 Column throughout the Chindit operations, was a son of the Regiment, having enlisted in 1922. He was commissioned in 1940 and on retirement from the Army in 1948 acted as Regimental Secretary until 1958.

Captain Pete Edwards (centre, in hat), the transport officer of 41 Column, with others of the 2nd Battalion, Burma, April 1944. Note the two Indian elephants used for the short time by the Column. The animal transport officer of 41 Column, Lieutenant Leyland, was evacuated with a fractured skull after being hit by a free drop from a supply aircraft on 6 April 1944.

A group of 41 Column 2nd Battalion in Burma in late April 1944. Seated on the left is Lance-Corporal Albert Halsall, who, a few weeks later, was to win the Military Medal. He commanded a Vickers machine-gun team covering the withdrawal of the Battalion from 'Blackpool Block' on 24 May 1944. Three of the gun crew were killed, but Halsall continued to operate the gun until the task was completed.

The RAF Sergeant Wireless Operator of 41 Column at his set in Burma, April 1944. Each Column had one RAF wireless operator and a radio for calling in supply drops, reinforcements and aircraft to evacuate the wounded.

A Chindit and mule of 41 Column 2nd Battalion, Burma, April 1944. The cardboard cartons on the ground to his right contain American 'K' rations, while behind him is one of the tin boxes containing a seven-day ration-pack. All the mules and ponies with the Columns had their vocal cords cut to prevent them giving away a position to the enemy. A former member of 46 Column's 'recce' platoon recalls having to dye his aptly-named pony 'Silver' with potassium permanganate and coffee-grains to camouflage it before flying into Burma.

Officers of 41 Column 2nd Battalion, Burma, April 1944. From left to right: Major V. F. Royle, Captain Winmill, Captain Charles Stock, Lieutenant-Colonel A. W. Thompson MC (CO), Lieutenant Coleman, Captain Gibb (MO), Lieutenant Harrison, Captain Tucker, Lieutenant Shaw. Major Royle took over command of the Battalion when Lieutenant-Colonel Thompson was wounded during the fighting in 'Blackpool Block' to the west of Myitkyina in May 1944.

Officer POWs of the 1st Battalion in Oflag 79 (VIIIF) at Brunswick (Braunschweig), Querum, Germany, May 1944. Left to right, back row: Lieutenant Constable, Lieutenant Mitchell, Captain Hands, Lieutenant Wingrove, Lieutenant Roberts, Lieutenant Harvey, Lieutenant King. Front row: Captain McKenzie, Lieutenant & QM Spiers, Major Tilly, Lieutenant Horne, Lieutenant Griffin. Wingrove and Roberts were taken prisoner in the Western Desert in June 1942, the remainder on Leros in November 1943.

General Montgomery inspects men of 107th Regiment RAC (King's Own) accompanied by the Commanding Officer, Lieutenant-Colonel H. H. K. Rowe, at Dover in February 1944. The Regiment embarked for Normandy on 30 June and 1 July 1944. *IWM H35669*

Soldiers of the 1st Battalion in Umbertide, 20 miles north of Perugia, Italy, which they had just liberated, July 1944. *IWM NA16663*

Soldiers of the 1st Battalion 'mopping up' in Umbertide, July 1944. *IWM NA16661*

Privates Charles Savage and Frank Turner of the 1st Battalion firing at enemy positions across the River Tevere, Umbertide, Italy, July 1944. *IWM NA16659.*

Soldiers of the 1st Battalion on the road to Montone, about 4 miles south of Umbertide, July 1944 — it always seems to be the smallest man in the section who carries the bren-gun! The Battalion captured the village of Montone on 7 July, after a night march of 12 miles, in a dawn attack without artillery support. After several hours of hard house-to-house fighting, the village was taken. The commanding officer, Lt Col Anderson, was awarded an immediate DSO for his leadership in this action. *IWM NA16753*

Two jeeps carrying the tactical headquarters of the 1st Battalion, Tiber Valley, Italy, 1944. The driver of the first jeep is Private Fitzgerald and behind him are Lieutenant-Colonel Bunbury, the Commanding Officer (left), and the Adjutant, Captain Brigden. Bunbury, originally commissioned into the Duke of Wellington's Regiment in 1930, joined the 8th Battalion on Malta as Second-in-Command in 1943, was acting CO from the summer of 1944 and officially from October 1944 to October 1945. He received the DSO for his leadership of the Battalion in Italy and a bar to the DSO whilst commanding the 1st Battalion of the Dukes in 1953 at the Battle of the Hook in Korea.

Churchill Tanks of C Squadron, 107th Regiment RAC (King's Own), moving up for the attack on Hill 112 near Caen, Normandy, on 15 July 1944. This was the Regiment's first action after landing in France. The leading tank is equipped with a 95mm close-support gun. *IWM B7585*

Lieutenant Fothergill watches members of the crew of his tank 'BRITON' cleaning the Besa machine-gun, B Squadron, 107th Regiment RAC (King's Own), Normandy, July 1944. Fothergill was killed in action on 14 August 1944. Most of the Regiment's tanks were given names which began with the letter of the Squadron, A, B or C; two of HQ Squadron's tanks were named 'LANCASTER' and 'LION'. 'LION', the Commanding Officer's tank, covered 1,900 miles on its tracks before leaving the Regiment. *IWM B7624*

Major Hugh Davies briefs his troop leaders of 107th Regiment RAC (King's Own), Normandy, July 1944. The Regiment wore the King's Own cap-badge (white-metal or chromed) in the black tank beret and a lion badge in blue and gold on the sleeve of the battledress. Major Davies, a regular King's Own officer, won a Military Cross for his leadership of B Squadron during operations in a small bridgehead across the River Orne, opposite Brieux and Grimbosq south of Caen on 8 August. The 11 tanks, which crossed the ford over the river, were eventually reduced to two after putting up a tremendous fight. Major Davies's own tank was knocked out; he rescued the wounded gunner and made several unsuccessful attempts to recover the body of his driver from the wreck. Major Davies later became a Brigadier and Colonel of the Queen's Own Hussars. *IWM B7629*

Thirteen Churchill tanks of 107th Regiment RAC (King's Own) knocked out during the heavy fighting on the Orne on 7–8 August 1944, photographed in a field at Brieux, Normandy, in 1947. Tanks from A and C Squadrons faced a counter-attack by two columns of German armour whilst supporting 176th Brigade of 59th Division at this small bridgehead, and were joined by B Squadron on 8 August. The Regiment lost a total of 22 tanks, 17 of which were a total loss.

A Churchill tank of B Squadron 107th Regiment RAC (King's Own) undergoes track repairs during operations in the River Orne bridgehead, Normandy, August 1944. Behind is a turretless Churchill Armoured Recovery Vehicle. *IWM B9162*

A Stuart light tank of HQ Squadron, 107th Regiment RAC (King's Own), crossing the Antwerp-Turnhout Canal at Ryckevorsel, northern Belgium, in October 1944. The Recce Troop of HQ Squadron was equipped with these American light tanks. *IWM B11111*

Churchill tanks of B Squadron 107th Regiment RAC (King's Own) travelling through Ryckevorsel in the same month. The tank 'BRAZEN', complete with lucky horseshoe, is in the foreground. *IWM B11115*

The troop leaders tank of No 3 Troop, C Squadron, 107th Regiment RAC (King's Own), *en route* by tank transporter from Oudenbosch to Budel in Holland in November 1944. Standing, left to right, are Trooper Morgan, Lieutenant Spratt and Trooper Lovell, with Corporal Forster on the tank. Most of 34th Armoured Brigade moved from St Omer near the Belgian border across Belgium to the Eindhoven area in early October; this was the first time that the tanks had moved by their transporters since landing in Normandy. C Squadron was made up from the remnants of 153 Regiment RAC (Essex Regiment), which was transferred to 107th on disbandment in August 1944.

Soldiers of B Company 1st Battalion coming out of action on Pideura Ridge, west of Faenza, to spend Christmas at Forlinpopoli, Italy, 20 December 1944. The Battalion successfully defended its positions and eventually secured the whole of the ridge against strong enemy opposition, which included counter-attacks by the German 90th Light Division, against which the 1st Battalion had fought in the Western Desert in 1942.

One of C Squadron's 95mm gun close-support tanks bogged down in the Ardennes, January 1945. *IWM B13443*

The crew of 'ARKHOLME', named after the village near Lancaster, reading the mail. A Squadron 107th Regiment RAC (King's Own), Reichswald Forest, Germany, February 1945. *IWM B14424*

'Lancaster' Bailey Bridge across the River Savio, San Carlo, northern Italy, captured by the 1st Battalion in November 1944.

A 3-inch mortar position of the 1st Battalion on the Senio Front, northern Italy, January 1945.

Chapter 9

1945-80

SUSPENSION, AMALGAMATION AND REBIRTH

Following the end of hostilities, units of the Regiment were scattered all over the world. The 1st Battalion, still in 10th Indian Division, was at Ferrara in northern Italy. The 2nd and 7th Battalions were at Cawnpore and Bangalore in India, whilst 107th Regiment RAC (King's Own) was in Germany, and 56 Anti-Tank Regiment RA (King's Own) in Burma. Gradually these were reduced by demobilisation and disbandment in late 1945 and early 1946, until only the two Regular and 7th Battalions remained.

At the end of 1945 the 1st Battalion moved to Bolzano in the Italian Tyrol, and in early 1946 transferred to 24th Guards Brigade in 56th (London) Division at Trieste, in the disputed zone on the Yugoslav frontier. Apart from a brief period in Sesena and Pola in late 1946, it was based in Rosetti Barracks, Trieste. During this period the training and fitness of the Battalion was brought up to a high standard by the Commanding Officer, Lieutenant-Colonel W. V. H. Robins DSO.

The 2nd Battalion remained in India, based at Cawnpore and finally at Calcutta until October 1947, carrying out internal security duties prior to India's Independence. On the disbandment of the 7th Battalion in April 1947, some men were transferred to the 2nd Battalion. On 28 October the

latter went to Egypt, followed in January 1948 by a move to Eritrea. Based at Asmara, the Battalion's role was to maintain law and order in the British Military-administered former Italian colony.

Whilst at Asmara the 2nd Battalion received notice that it was to be placed in suspended animation, which effectively meant disbandment, as part of the reductions in the size of the Regular Army. In January 1949 it moved to Khartoum in the Sudan; drafts of men were sent to bring the 1st Battalion up to strength and the surplus were sent to other Lancastrian Brigade Units. On 15 March the last 'Retreat' was sounded and on the 17th the Cadre left to join the 1st Battalion in Trieste, where the Amalgamation Parade was held on St George's Day 1949. The 2nd Battalion's Colours were retained by the 1st until 1955, when they were laid up in the King's Chapel, Gibraltar, representing the Regiment's service on 'the Rock' in 1704–5.

In 1947 the Territorial Army units of the Regiment were reconstituted. In the Furness area 380th Light Anti-Tank Regiment RA (King's Own) (TA) in Barrow, Ulverston and Dalton replaced 56th Anti-Tank Regiment. The pre-war 5th Battalion (TA) was reformed, with Headquarters and Companies at Phoenix Street, Lancaster, and Companies at Morecambe, Carnforth and Fleetwood. Both units had a percentage of volunteers, but soon began to receive National Servicemen who completed their period of engagement with the TA. The Territorials were a regular sight within the Regimental area, providing troops for Mayoral and Armistice Day Parades and two Royal Visits to Lancaster by HM King George VI in 1951 and HM Queen Elizabeth II in 1955. Detachments were also present at the 1953 Coronation.

The 1st Battalion remained in Trieste until April 1950, when it returned to England, first to Hadrian's Camp, Carlisle, and then to Saighton Camp, Chester, where it acted as the Lancastrian Brigade Training Battalion. It moved to Bulford Camp in February 1951 and then to Osnabruck in West Germany, as part of 6th Armoured Division, in December. Lieutenant-Colonel W. P. Scott DSO MC, King's Regiment, took over the Battalion from Lieutenant-Colonel W. M. W. Cooper; he had previously commanded a King's Regiment Battalion in the Chindit Campaign in Burma, in which the 2nd Battalion King's Own had also taken part. During this period the Battalion sent men as drafts to other units in Korea, then on 8 September 1953 the Battalion itself embarked for service there to join 29th Commonwealth Infantry Brigade as part of the UN peace-keeping force based in Korea during the peace negotiations. Prior to this a representative detachment from the Battalion went to Lancaster on 29 August 1953 for the conferment of the Freedom of the City on the Regiment. Groups from the TA, Home Guard, WRAC, Regimental Association and Cadets also took part.

After almost a year in Korea the Battalion moved to Hong Kong in September 1954 for a two-year posting as part of 48th Gurkha Infantry Brigade. It returned home to Harrington Barracks at Formby in August 1956, followed by a move to Deerbolt Camp, Barnard Castle, in January 1957, where it joined 24th Independent Infantry Brigade. Lieutenant-Colonel Scott handed over the Battalion in Hong Kong to Lieutenant-Colonel J. B. L. Underwood, who in turn was succeeded by Lieutenant-Colonel C. H. Lincoln. In July 1958 the Battalion arrived in Kenya, but after a few days was ordered to Aden and Bahrain due to the political unrest in the colony. It spent the next 3½ months carrying out internal security duties, mainly guarding installations in the colony. Some training was possible and a composite 'Patrol' company

spent a month in the mountain area near Lauder. Officers and men of this company qualified for the General Service Medal with clasp 'Arabian Peninsula'. In October the Battalion returned to Kenya and was based at Gil Gil camp, near Nakuru.

In July 1957 it was announced that The King's Own would amalgamate with its neighbour The Border Regiment as part of the next stage in the reduction of the British Army. The Colonels of the two Regiments and their committees worked hard to ensure that this would happen as smoothly as possible, and in addition officers and NCOs were cross-posted between the Regiments. Perhaps the first blow to independence was the loss of the treasured lion cap-badge at the Depot in July 1958, when the Lancastrian Brigade cap-badge was taken into use; the 1st Battalion did not rebadge until it returned from Kenya in 1959, while the TA and Cadets continued to be badged King's Own. The creation of the Lancastrian Brigade and the centralisation of training at Fulwood Barracks, Preston, led to the closure of the Regimental Depot, Bowerham Barracks, on 26 September 1959, the same day that the 1st Battalion held its Farewell Parade in Lancaster.

On 1 October the King's Own Royal Border Regiment came into being. On its return from Kenya in July 1959, the 1st Battalion was based at Westwick Camp, Barnard Castle; the 1st Battalion of the Border Regiment were nearby at Humbleton Camp. The official Amalgamation Parade and Presentation of New Colours thus took place at Westwick Camp on 31 October. The Regimental Headquarters of the new Regiment was based initially in the Commanding Officer's house at Bowerham, but later moved into Regimental House on Coulston Road nearby. In 1962 the Church of England authorities bought the Barracks, which became St Martin's Teacher Training College. Many of the old buildings were retained, including the keep, barrack-blocks, married quarters, drill shed, officer's mess and stores, but they were converted to new uses. No doubt the spirit of many a former Depot Regimental Sergeant Major looks very unfavourably at the new buildings constructed on the sacred barrack square!

The Regiment continued to survive through the 5th Battalion (TA), which was built up to strength by a major recruiting drive conducted by the Commanding Officer, Lieutenant-Colonel N. St G.

Gribbon, from 1959. Ulverston, the pre-war Headquarters of the 4th Battalion (TA) and which had been closed since 1955 when 380th Light Regiment RA (King's Own) TA had been reduced to a single Battery (R) at Barrow, was reactivated and Furness included in the Battalion area. The Battalion absorbed the Battery personnel from Barrow in 1960 and in 1961 was redesignated the 4/5th Battalion King's Own Royal Regiment (Lancaster), with companies at Fleetwood, Morecambe and Carnforth, Ulverston and Barrow and Headquarters at Lancaster. Thereafter the Battalion, admirably supported by its Band and Corps of Drums, maintained a high profile in the Regimental area.

In the same year the links with the area were further strengthened by the presentation of new drums to the 4/5th Battalion by the civic authorities, companies, organisations and private subscribers from Fleetwood to Barrow. In June 1962 the Battalion received new Colours from Lord Derby.

However, as the result of cuts in the Territorial Army in April 1967, 4/5th Battalion suffered reductions in manpower and resources. The Ulverston and Morecambe Companies were disbanded and the personnel transferred to Barrow and Lancaster. A third Company was created by merging the Fleetwood Company with the Blackpool Gunners (formerly R battery 288 LAA Regiment RA TA). On 1 April 1969 the Battalion was reduced to a Cadre of eight all ranks, which formed the nucleus of the Battalion should it need to be re-formed. The new Territorial Army and Volunteer Reserve (TAVR) Unit in Lancashire was the Lancastrian Volunteers, formed on 1 April 1967. 'E' Company, formed at Lancaster on 1 April 1969,

absorbed some of the former 4/5th Battalion personnel from Lancaster and Barrow.

Eventually it was decided to restore the system of Territorial Battalions of the Line Regiments in the North West. On 27 April 1975 the inaugural parade of the 4th (Volunteer) Battalion King's Own Royal Border Regiment (TAVR) was held in Lancaster. The Colours of the 4/5th Battalion King's Own, which had been carried by the Cadre of the 4/5th Battalion and 'E' Company Lancastrian Volunteers, were re-dedicated and taken into use, and the new Battalion absorbed former members of the 4/5th Battalion's Cadre and Lancastrian and Northumbrian Volunteers from Lancaster, Kendal, Barrow, Workington and Carlisle.

In the same year Regimental Headquarters moved from Lancaster to more suitable accommodation in the former Border Regiment's Depot Officers' Mess at Carlisle Castle. Moreover, the Regimental Associations of The King's Own and Border Regiments merged to form the King's Own Royal Border Regimental Association. The Amalgamation was now complete and the new Regiment and its family, incorporating the customs, traditions and history of its two famous predecessors, was truly born.

On 11 July 1980 the 1st and 4th Battalions King's Own Royal Border Regiment paraded at Weeton Camp near Blackpool to celebrate the Regiment's Tercentenary and receive new Colours from the Colonel-in-Chief, HRH Princess Alexandra, and formally paraded the old Colours of the 4/5th Battalion for the last time. Two days later, on 13 July 1980, they were laid up in the King's Own Regimental Chapel in Lancaster, 300 years to the day since the Regiment had been raised.

C Company 7th Battalion at Bangalore, India, in November 1946.

Corporal Bates and Capt Meecham of the 2nd Battalion search passengers from a bus during internal security duties in Calcutta, India, in August 1947.

Officers of the 2nd Battalion at Cawnpore, India, February 1947. Left to right, back row: 2/Lt P. Kellett, 2/Lt P. Bromilow, 2/Lt M. H. Baldwin, 2/Lt P. Goddard, Lt I. Blenkinsop, 2/Lt H. Earp, Lt J. Warham. Middle row: Lt P. Meecham, Lt J. Rodger, Lt St J. Newman, Lt R. Ashworth, Capt C. Foster, Capt D. Morton (RAMC), Lt D. Harper, Lt P. Bennett, Lt H. Scott. Front row: Capt M. Round, Maj J. Paton, Capt K. Williams, Lt Col H. Creedon (CO), Maj C. Jones, Capt M. Darkes (QM), Capt A. Annesley.

A patrol of the 2nd Battalion commanded by 2/Lt D. E. Dunand in Asmara, Eritrea, 1948.

Major-General R. M. Luckcock CB CMG DSO, Colonel of the Regiment, presents the Regimental Colour to Lieutenant A. Church during the new Colours presentation to the 1st Battalion at San Sabba Stadium, Trieste, on 25 July 1947. In the centre, from left to right, are Rev Newman, Maj J. Wickham, Lt G. Farmer (King's Colour), the Colonel of the Regiment, Lt A. Church, Lt Col W. V. H. Robins DSO, Maj N. St G. Gribbon, Rev Howard.

Field Marshal Viscount Montgomery of Alamein KG GCB DSO inspects a Guard-of-Honour during his inspection of the 1st Battalion at Rosetti Barracks, Trieste, on 3 July 1948. He is accompanied by Major-General T. S. Airey CB CBE and the Guard Commander Captain D. J. Martin.

The Amalgamation Parade of the 1st and 2nd Battalions at San Sabba Stadium, Trieste, on St George's Day 1949. Brigadier J. H. Hardy CBE MC, the Colonel of the Regiment, salutes as the Escort to the 1st and 2nd Battalions' Regimental Colours, commanded by Major T. Leahy, marches past.

The Mayor of Morecambe and Heysham, Councillor Edgar Bell, inspects the WRAC (TA) contingent at Morecambe on Mayoral Sunday in 1951, accompanied by Major D. B. Long MC, the officer commanding B Company 5th Battalion (TA). Note the King's Own cap-badge worn by the WRACs on the battledress blouse. The Company was based at the West End Road Drill Hall which opened in 1937, closed in 1967 and is now occupied by the Salvation Army.

The 1st Battalion's Annual Administration Inspection at Osnabruck, Germany, on St George's Day 1952.

The Band of the 2nd Battalion playing at Old Trafford, Manchester, during the second day of the Test Match between England and the Australian XI, 21 August 1945. During the war this band, under the direction of Bandmaster Basil Brown, gave numerous public performances and was often heard on the radio. Sadly, no band of the King's Own ever made any recordings of its music.

The Band of the 5th Battalion (TA) leads the Battalion up Cheapside in Lancaster *en route* to the Castle Station for Annual Camp, August 1952.

South Africa barrack-room, Brooke Block, Bowerham Barracks, 1951. Compare this with the views on p43 and p108.

Brigadier J. H. Hardy CBE MC, Colonel of the Regiment, receives the Scroll conferring the Freedom of the City of Lancaster from the Mayor, Councillor N. B. Gorrill, on 29 August 1953. Looking on are Captain J. M. Hardy, Major J. Wickham, Officer Commanding Regimental Depot, Lieutenant-Colonel Boissier-Wyles TD, Commanding Officer of the 5th Battalion (TA), and on the right Mr R. M. Middleton OBE, the Town Clerk.

The Colour Party and No 3 Guard of the 1st Battalion pass the saluting base at the Town Hall, as the Regiment exercises its Freedom Rights of marching through the City of Lancaster with drums beating, bands playing, colours flying and bayonets fixed, on 29 August 1953. The Freedom Rights were re-conferred on The King's Own Royal Border Regiment on St George's Day 1960.

B Company 1st Battalion on Kamak San, Korea, 1954. The Battalion was based at Teal Bridge Camp on the 38th Parallel near the valley of the River Imjin. On arrival it was issued with a whole new range of equipment and clothing including '44 pattern webbing, combat dress, parkas and heavy-duty cold-wet-weather boots.

CSM R. Taylor presents roses to men of A Company, 1st Battalion, St George's Day, Korea, 1954. All ranks who served in Korea received the United Nations Korea Medal. Those members of the Regiment who served with other units such as the Gloucestershire and King's Regiments in Korea, between 1951 and June 1953, were also entitled to the Queen's Korea Medal.

The 1st Battalion arrives in Hong Kong, 20 September 1954. In the foreground are, from the left, CSMs Brickell, Taylor, Eyre and Charnley.

Machine-gunners from S Company 1st Battalion using four-legged and mechanised transport in Hong Kong, 1955.

The 1st Battalion Trooping the Colour on St George's Day, Hong Kong, 1955. This was the first occasion that a Regiment carried out a trooping with the new FN rifle, which had been adopted by the Army. Major A. Collis commanded the Escort to the Colour, Captain D. E. Dunand acted as Captain of the Escort, and Lieutenant I. E. Bishop carried the Regimental Colour. The salute was taken by Lieutenant-General C. S. Sugden CB CBE, Commander British Forces Hong Kong.

Types of uniform worn by the Regiment at home and abroad, Hong Kong, 1956. From the left: Fifer (Ceremonial Order), Private (Battle Order), Private (Shirt Sleeve Order), Sergeant (No 1 Dress), Private (No 3 Dress), Corporal (Drill Order), Lance-Corporal (Walking Out Order), and Drummer (Summer Ceremonial).

The Royal Visit to Lancaster on 13 April 1955. HM Queen Elizabeth II inspects a Guard-of-Honour provided by the 5th Battalion (TA) in Dalton Square, Lancaster. Her Majesty is accompanied by Major A. Preston TD, following behind is the Commanding Officer, Lieutenant-Colonel G. Harvey, and on the right of the guard is CSM H. Gardner MBE.

Colonel E. J. Barton-Harrison, the Assistant County Commandant, presents the News of the World Shooting Cup to the Lancaster Detachment of the 1/5th King's Own Cadet Battalion at the Drill Hall, Phoenix Street, Lancaster, on 8 March 1955. The detachment Commander, Major Les Heap (on the left), looks on. A King's Own Army Cadet unit was formed in Lancaster during the First World War and wore a distinctive shoulder-title 1/C/KING'S OWN. The unit appears to have been disbanded in the early 1920s, but since the formation of the Army Cadet Force during the Second World War there have always been cadet units affiliated to the Regiment.

The staff of the Regimental Depot, Bowerham Barracks, Lancaster, 1956. Left to right, front row: CSM J. Heath, unknown, Lt A. Booth, Capt G. Hill, Maj R. J. T. Evans (CO), Maj (QM) D. Gibb DCM, Capt E. Turton, unknown, RSM G. Hull, QMSI J. Lockwood. Second row: Sgt Hamer, unknown, Sgt Brooks, unknown, Sgt Smith, C/Sgt Mitchell, Sgt Mills, C/Sgt Smith, Sgt Hammond, unknown, Sgt Battle, Sgt Waters, Sgt Woodward.

In December 1946 the Depot was re-activated as No 4 Primary Training Centre, which provided National Service recruits with their six weeks basic training. Training ceased in March 1948, when the Lancastrian Brigade Training Centre was opened in Carlisle. Bowerham Barracks was then occupied by the 18th Medium Regiment Royal Artillery until late 1951, when the Depot was reactivated once more. The last National Servicemen passed out of the Depot in February 1959.

Men of the 1st Battalion practice loading vehicles into aircraft at Deerbolt Camp, Barnard Castle, 1957.

A display of weapons and signalling equipment at the Regimental Depot during an open-day for parents in March 1957. Sergeant G. Ellwood stands fourth from left, and Lieutenant P. Blincoe sixth from right.

Men of C Company 1st Battalion with Centurion tanks of B Squadron 16/5th Lancers, during a demonstration of Infantry-Tank Co-operation at the Northern Command CCF Camp at Gandale, North Yorkshire, in July 1957.

Officers of the 1st Battalion at Barnard Castle, 1957. Left to right, back row: Lt Norcross, Lt Keir, Lt Bishop, Lt Teague, Lt Pearson, 2/Lt Pheysey, 2/Lt Hurley, Capt Hilton, Lt Smith, 2/Lt Tittle, Lt (QM) Lamour MM. Centre row: Capt Foster, Maj Evans, Maj Weir MC, Maj Gribbon, the Commanding Officer, Lt-Col Lincoln, Capt Roberts, Maj Murphy, Maj Roberts, Maj Smalley. Front row: 2/Lts Manktelow, Ireland, Fox, Walters, Calderbank, Langdon and Evans.

Retreat being sounded at the Regimental Depot on the anniversary of the Battle of Waterloo, 18 June 1957. As the Regimental Flag is lowered, Drummer Garrity sounds 'Retreat' on a bugle used at Waterloo, having beaten the 'Drummer's Call' on a drum carried by the Regiment during the Napoleonic Wars.

Machine-gunners of D Company 1st Battalion climb the Amudah Pass near Lauder, in Audhali State, Western Protectorate of Aden, during donkey trials in October 1958. The donkeys were being tested for their suitability as pack animals for the Vickers machine-guns, 3-inch mortars and pioneer equipment of the Support Platoons over some of the worst terrain in the world.

Filling water-bowsers during field training, 1st Battalion, Kenya, 1959.

Major-General Anderson CB CBE DSO, **the Colonel of the Regiment, accompanied by the Mayor of Lancaster, Councillor Mrs C. Pickard, Lt P. E. Dew, Lt-Col Lincoln** OBE, **Major Dockerill** MBE **and RSM R. Taylor** MBE, **inspects men of the 1st Battalion at the Regiment's Farewell Parade prior to amalgamation on Giant Axe Field, Lancaster, on 26 September 1959.**

The 1st Battalion marches along Brock Street, Lancaster, as it approaches the Town Hall during the Farewell Parade.

The King's Own Old Comrades in front of Lancaster Castle after their church service on the day following the 1st Battalion's Farewell Parade through the City. In the centre is Major-General Anderson CB CBE DSO, the Colonel of the Regiment, flanked by the Regimental Seretary, Brigadier Billy Burke DSO (left) and Major Freddie Parker (right), the Assistant Regimental Secretary.

The Old Colours of The King's Own and Border Regiments are trooped through the ranks for the last time to the strains of 'Auld Lang Syne' at the Amalgamation Parade, Westwick Camp, Barnard Castle, Co Durham, on 31 October 1959. The Queen's Colours of The King's Own and Border Regiments were carried by 2/Lt R. A. Parker and Lt G. A. M. Nash, the Regimental Colours by 2/Lt R. Sibbick and Lt D. B. Lewthwaite. Lt J. H. Milburn and Lt I. P. Hurley had the honour of receiving and carrying the new Colours of the 1st Battalion King's Own Royal Border Regiment which were presented by the Chief of the Imperial General Staff, General Sir Francis Festing GCB KCB DSO.

Drum-Major R. Rogerson and the Drums of the 4/5th Battalion (TA) parade behind Lancaster Castle on St George's Day 1961. This was the first public appearance in Lancaster of the new drums which had been presented to the Battalion at a special ceremony held at Bowerham Barracks on 22 April. The drums were presented by Lancaster City Council, Morecambe and Heysham Corporation, Lancaster Rural District Council, the people of Barrow and Ulverston, by private subscription and by Lansil Limited, Jas Williamson & Son Ltd, Glaxo Laboratories Ltd, Storey Bros Ltd, Waring and Gillow Ltd, with Nelsons Silk Ltd, Nelson Acetate Ltd, Standfast Dyers and Printers Ltd, and West End Social Club, Fleetwood. During Annual Camp at Stanford, Middlesex, in June 1964 the Band and Drums, together with the other Bands of 42nd East Lancashire Division (TA), beat 'Retreat' on Horse Guards Parade in London, the first time that a Territorial Division had done so.

Lord Derby MC JP presents the new Regimental Colour of the 4/5th Battalion (TA) to Captain Wollaston, at the New Colours Parade on Giant Axe Field, Lancaster, 30 June 1962. Captain Clarke received the Queen's Colour. The Regiment established a record in that the 4/5th Battalion was the first TA unit to Troop the Colour with the FN rifle, the 1st Battalion having been the first Regular Army unit to do so in Hong Kong in 1955. The standard of the soldiers on parade was so high that one guest commented to the Commanding Officer that 'it was very kind of the 1st Battalion to loan the men for the parade'.

A group from the 4/5th Battalion (TA) on exercise in Germany in April 1965. From the left: L/Cpl Cox, Sgt Hodgson, L/Cpl Rigby, Cpl Thompson, Cpl Rossiter, Sgt Burgess and 2/Lt C. Warren. A composite platoon under 2/Lt Warren went to Munster for a fortnight's training with the 1st Battalion Queen's Royal Surrey Regiment; he was later commissioned into the 1st Battalion King's Own Royal Border Regiment.

Men from the anti-tank platoon of B Company 4/5th Battalion (TA) man-handling a BAT anti-tank gun during Annual Camp at Plasterdown in Devon, June 1966. From the left: Cpl Dunning, Pte Maguire, Pte Swithenbank, Pte E. Dawson and Cpl Peters. B Company was based at the West End Road Drill Hall, Morecambe.

The Colours of the 4/5th Battalion King's Own Royal Regiment carried by the Colour Party of the 4th (Volunteer) Battalion King's Own Royal Border Regiment (TAVR) at the Battalion's inaugural parade in Lancaster on 27 April 1975. Led by Captain C. Arnison, Captain P. R. Bradburn carries the Queen's Colour and Captain M. G. Diss the Regimental Colour. The Escorts are CSM J. S. Byrne, S/Sgt R. Cardy and Sgt S. Eccles. These Colours were replaced at the Tercentenary Parade at Weeton Camp on 11 July 1980 and were laid up in the Regimental Chapel on 13 July, 300 years to the day since the Regiment was raised.

Appendix 1

TITLES AND BADGES
OF THE REGIMENT

Titles

1680	The Second Tangier Regiment or the Earl of Plymouth's Regiment of Foot for Tangier
1684	The Duchess of York and Albany's Regiment of Foot
1685	The Queen's Regiment of Foot
1703	The Queen's Regiment of Marines, or Royal Regiment of Marines
1710	The Queen's Own Regiment of Foot
1715	The King's Own Regiment of Foot
1743	Alternative title of 4th Foot
1751	4th Regiment or King's Own Royal Regiment of Foot
1752	Fourth (or The King's Own) Regiment of Foot
1865	4th (or King's Own Royal) Regiment of Foot
1881	The King's Own (Royal Lancaster Regiment)
1920	The King's Own Royal Regiment (Lancaster)

Badges

The Lion of England
The King's Own Royal Regiment and its successor The King's Own Royal Border Regiment are the only Regiments in the British Army to have worn this as their badge. It is a Regimental tradition that William III granted the badge in recognition of the Regiment being one of the first to ally with him when he landed at Torbay in 1688. It is also possible that it was granted as a reward for the Regiment's loyalty to William and Mary during their reign. It is first referred to in the Royal Warrant of 1751 as the Regiment's 'Ancient badge'.

A Lion first appears on the Regimental Colour of 1751, but the Lion of England was first used as a badge *circa* 1774 on the officers and other ranks shoulder belt-plates, on the shako-plate from 1800, on the buttons from *circa* 1808 and on the officers forage-cap from 1834. From 1872 it was worn as a collar-badge and from 1896 as the Regiment's cap-badge.

The Royal Cypher
The Royal Cypher is also first referred to in the Royal Warrant of 1751, which authorised the Regiment to bear 'In the centre of their colours the King's Cipher on a red ground within the garter and crown over it . . .'

The Red Rose of Lancaster
This was originally worn by the 1st Royal Lancashire Militia and adopted by The King's Own in 1881. It was worn below the lion on the old forage cap, appeared on the officer's waist belt-plate, and on the uniform buttons.

Appendix 2

COLONELS OF THE REGIMENT

Line Battalions

1680	Charles Earl of Plymouth
1680	Hon Piercy Kirke
1682	Colonel Charles Trelawny
1688	Colonel Sir Charles Orby
1688	Major-General Charles Trelawny (reinstated)
1692	Brigadier-General Henry Trelawny
1702	Lieutenant-General William Seymour
1717	Colonel The Hon Henry Berkeley
1719	The Hon Charles Cadogan
1734	Lieutenant-General William Barrell
1749	Colonel Robert Rich
1756	Lieutenant-General Alexander Duroure
1765	Colonel The Hon Robert Brudenell
1768	General Studholme Hodgson
1782	Major-General Sir John Burgoyne
1792	General George Morrison
1799	General John Pitt, 2nd Earl of Chatham KG
1835	General John Hodgson
1846	General Sir Thomas Bradford GCB GCH
1853	General Sir John Bell KCB
1876	General Studholme John Hodgson
1890	General William Sankey
1892	General William Wilby CB
1894	General Sir William Gordon Cameron KCB VD
1913	General Sir Archibald Hunter GCB GCVO DSO LLD TD
1926	Lieutenant-General Sir Oswald C. Borrett KCB CMG CBE DSO
1945	Major-General Russell M. Luckcock CB CMG DSO
1947	Brigadier John H. Hardy CBE MC
1957–1959	Major-General Richard N. Anderson CB CBE DSO

Royal Lancashire Militia, Militia, Volunteer and Territorial Battalions

1689	William George Richard, 9th Earl of Derby
1715	Philip Hoghton
1745	Edward, 11th Earl of Derby
1760	James Smith Stanley, Viscount Strange
1772	Edward, 12th Earl of Derby
1783	Thomas Stanley
1817	Peter Pattern Bold
1819	John Plumbe-Tempest
1852	John Talbot Clifton
1871	William Assheton Cross
1883	Duke of Devonshire (1st Volunteer Bn)
1886	The Rt Hon Lord Stanley of Preston (3rd Militia Bn)
1886	The Rt Hon The Earl of Derby (4th Militia Bn)
1901	General Sir Archibald Hunter KCB DSO (2nd Volunteer Bn)
1906	Lord Richard Cavendish (1st Volunteer Bn)
1908	Brigadier-General B. N. North CB MVO (3rd Special Reserve/Militia Bn) until his death in 1936

1908 The Rt Hon Lord Richard Cavendish CB CMG (4th Territorial Bn)

1908 General Sir Archibald Hunter GCB GCVO DSO TD LLD (5th Territorial Bn)

1932 The Rt Hon The Earl of Derby KG PC GCB GCVO TD (5th Territorial Bn)

1947 Colonel W. H. B. R. Kennedy TD (4th Territorial Bn)

1948 General Sir Neil Methuen Ritchie KCB KBE DSO MC (5th Territorial Bn)

1958-1969 Colonel Vernon F. Royle ERD DL (4th/5th Territorial Bn)

Colonels-in-Chief

1903 17 March, HM King Edward VII until his death on 6 May 1910

1913 19 August, HM King George V until his death on 20 January 1936

Colonels of The King's Own Royal Border Regiment

1959 Major-General Val Blomfield CB DSO

1961 Lieutenant-General Sir Richard N. Anderson KCB CBE DSO

1971 General Sir William A. Scotter KCB OBE MC

1981 Major-General David E. Miller CB CBE MC

1988 to date Major-General Robert J. Hodges CB OBE

Colonel-in-Chief

1977 to date HRH Princess Alexandra, The Hon Lady Ogilvy GCVO

Lieutenant-General O. C. Borrett CB CMG CBE DSO, the Colonel of the Regiment (seated, centre front row), with officers, Warrant Officers and Sergeants of the 2nd Battalion at Blenheim Barracks, Aldershot, on 17 April 1936. General Borrett (1878-1950) was the son of Major-General H. C. Borrett (see p36) and joined the Regiment in 1898. He served in the Boer War, India and throughout the First World War for which he received the CMG, DSO and Bar, and Legion d'Honneur; he was made an ADC to the King in 1919. He later commanded the 2nd Battalion, a Brigade in Waziristan, for which he was made a CB and a CBE, and Brigades in India and China. Promoted Major-General in 1931, he was GOC 46th N Midland Division (TA), GOC British troops in China 1933-35, and in 1936 was made Lieutenant of the Tower of London. He was Knighted in 1937 and retired in 1938. He was Colonel of the Regiment from 19 November 1926 until 31 December 1944. Also in the photograph on the front row, left to right, are: Maj R. H. Welch DSO, Lt W. Bell MC, RQMS W. Hudson MM, Maj E. R. O'Connor MC, RSM G. Bowles DCM, Lt Col J. E. Packard MC, Gen Borrett, Maj V. L. de Cordova MC, Bd Mr B. Brown, Maj J. H. Hardy MC, ORQMS J. B. Evans, Capt F. R. L. Mears, CSM F. J. Parker.

Appendix 3

BATTLE HONOURS

The Regiment was granted its first Battle Honour CORUNNA in 1812. The earliest Honour, NAMUR 1695, was not granted until March 1910. Until after the First World War Battle Honours were borne on the Regimental Colour only. The following were awarded in the period up to 1914 and borne on the Regimental Colour:

NAMUR 1695, GIBRALTAR 1704–5, GUADELOUPE 1759, ST LUCIA 1778, CORUNNA, BADAJOZ, SALAMANCA, VITTORIA, ST SEBASTIAN, NIVE, PENINSULA, BLADENSBURG, WATERLOO, ALMA, INKERMAN, SEVASTOPOL, ABYSSINIA, SOUTH AFRICA 1879, RELIEF OF LADYSMITH, SOUTH AFRICA 1899–1902

The Colours of the Militia and Territorial Battalions were not emblazoned with the Regimental Battle Honours until after the First World War. However, the 1st Royal Lancashire Militia received the Honour MEDITERRANEAN for its service in the Ionian Islands during the Crimean War of 1855–56, and this was borne on the Regimental Colour of both Battalions. As the 3rd and 4th (Militia) Battalions King's Own (Royal Lancaster Regiment), they received the Honours SOUTH AFRICA 1900–02 and SOUTH AFRICA 1900–01 respectively for service during the Boer War.

The 4th (Territorial) and 5th (Territorial) Battalions both received the Honour SOUTH AFRICA 1900–02 in recognition of the service of the Volunteer Active Service Companies during the Boer War.

The First World War
The following Battle Honours were published in the 1st Battalion's orders on 14 March 1924. Those in CAPITALS were emblazoned on the King's Colour.

Le Cateau, Retreat from Mons, MARNE 1914, Aisne 1914, Armentieres 1914, YPRES 1915, '17, Gravenstafel, St Julien, Frezenburg, Bellewaarde, Festubert 1915, Loos, SOMME 1916, '18, Albert 1916–18, Bazentin, Delville Wood, Pozieres, Guillemont, Ginchy, Flers-Courcelette, Morval, Le Transloy, Ancre Heights, Ancre 1916, ARRAS 1917, '18, Scarpe 1917, '18, Arleux, MESSINES 1917, Pilckem, Menin Road, Polygon Wood, Broodseinde, Poelcappelle, Passchendaele, Cambrai 1917, '18, St Quentin, LYS, Estaries, Hazebrouck, Bethune, Bapaume 1918, Drocourt-Queant, Hindenburg Line, Canal du Nord, Selle, Valenciennes, Sambre, FRANCE & FLANDERS 1914–18, Struma, Doiran 1917–18, MACEDONIA 1915–18, Suvla, Sari Bair, GALLIPOLI 1915, Egypt 1916, Tigris 1916, Kut-al-Mara 1917, Baghdad, MESOPOTAMIA 1916–18.

The Second World War
The following Battle Honours were approved by the War Office in 1957. Those in CAPITALS were emblazoned on the Queen's Colour.

St Omer-La Bassee, DUNKIRK 1940, NORTH-WEST EUROPE 1940, DEFENCE OF HABBANIYA, Falluja, Iraq 1941, MERJAYUN, Jebel Mazar, Syria 1941, Tobruk 1941, TOBRUK SORTIE, NORTH AFRICA 1940–42, MONTONE, Citta di Castello, San Martino Sogliano, LAMONE BRIDGEHEAD, Italy 1944–45, MALTA 1941–42, CHINDITS 1944, Burma 1944.

The 5th Battalion (TA), which became 107th Regiment RAC (King's Own) during the war, received the Honorary Distinction of the mailed-fist badge of the Royal Armoured Corps, with the year dates 1944–45 and one scroll, 'NORTH-WEST-EUROPE', which was borne on the Regimental Colour. This Honour is also on the Regimental Colour of the successor unit, the 4th (Volunteer) Battalion The King's Own Royal Border Regiment (TAVR).

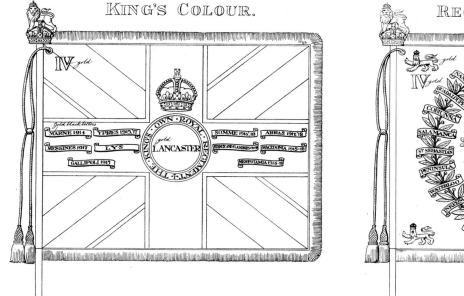
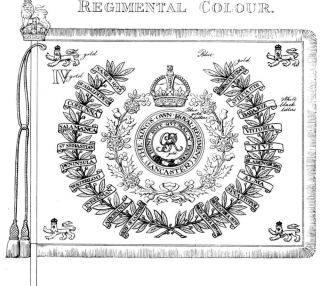

The design for the King's and Regimental Colours of the 4th Battalion (TA) King's Own Royal Regiment (Lancaster), which were refurbished in 1924, showing the Battle Honours up to 1914 (Regimental Colour) and ten from the First World War (King's Colour).

Appendix 4

RECIPIENTS OF THE VICTORIA CROSS AND THE GEORGE CROSS

The Crimean War, 1854–56

3319 Private Thomas Grady VC DCM, 4th (King's Own) Regiment of Foot

Private Thomas Grady, born at Cheddah in Galway, Ireland, in 1835, originally enlisted under age in the 99th Foot (2nd Battalion The Wiltshire Regiment) at Liverpool on 8 June 1853. He transferred to the 4th King's Own on 13 February 1854. Whilst serving in the trenches in front of Sebastopol during the Crimean War he was recommended for the Victoria Cross by Captain Lushington RN:

> For having, on the 18th October 1854, volunteered to repair the Embrazures of the Sailor's Battery on the left Attack, and effected the same, with the assistance of one other Volunteer, under a very heavy fire from a line of batteries.

Shortly afterwards Tom Grady received a second VC recommendation:

> For gallant conduct on the 22nd November 1854, in the repulse of the Russian attack on the advanced Trench on the Left Attack, when on being severely wounded, he refused to quit the front, encouraging, by such determined bearing, the weak force engaged with the Enemy to maintain its position.

The award to Grady of a VC and Bar would have been more appropriate, but the original VC warrant did not permit the award of a Bar for a second act of gallantry if the act occurred before the approval and presentation of the original VC. In this case both acts of gallantry were considered together by the War Office; the award was approved on 17 June 1857 and announced in the *London Gazette* of 23 June 1857. Grady also received the Distinguished Conduct Medal with a gratuity of £5, but no record survives of the citation.

He completed his service on 21 September 1856 and was discharged to pension, owing to his wounds, at Aldershot on 28 October 1856. He was decorated by Queen Victoria at the first VC presentation in Hyde Park on 26 June 1857 and later emigrated to Australia, where he died near Melbourne on 18 May 1891. Tom Grady's gallantry became firmly entrenched in Regimental folklore and tradition with the publication in about 1905 of a poem by Ellis Williams, a former Colour Sergeant in the Regiment, entitled 'How Tom Grady Cleared the Gun'. His Victoria Cross was donated by his family to the Australian War Memorial in Canberra in 1986.

The First World War, 1914–18

10210 Private Harry Christian VC, 2nd Battalion

Harry Christian was born on 17 January 1892 at Wallthwaite, Pennington, near Ulverston, and educated at the National School, Ulverston. In 1910 he enlisted in the 2nd Battalion King's Own and was serving in India at the outbreak of war. He returned home with his Battalion in December 1914 and proceeded immediately to France.

He was awarded the Victoria Cross for bravery on 15 October 1915 near Givenchy. The citation was published in the *London Gazette* on 3 March 1916:

> For most conspicuous bravery. He was holding a crater with five or six men in front of our trenches. The enemy commenced a very heavy bombardment of the position with heavy 'minenwerfer' bombs forcing a temporary withdrawal. When he found that three men were missing, Private Christian at once returned alone to the crater and, although bombs were continually bursting actually on the edge of the crater, he found, dug out, and carried one by one into safety all three men, thereby undoubtedly saving their lives. Later he placed himself where he could see the bombs coming, and directed his comrades when and where to seek cover.

Subsequently wounded, Christian returned to England and was still recuperating when King George V presented him with the VC in Glasgow in September 1917. He later rejoined his Battalion in Salonika and was discharged in 1919. For 40 years he was 'mine host' at the Park Head Inn at Egremont in Cumberland and was a staunch member of the Regimental Association. He died at Thornhill, Egremont, on 2 September 1974, aged 82. His medals are in the Regimental Museum.

12639 Private James Miller VC (Posthumous), 7th (Service) Battalion

James Miller was born on 13 March 1890 at Taylor's Farm, Hoghton, near Preston, the son of George and Mary Miller. The family later moved to 1 Ollerton Terrace, Withnell, near Chorley, and James worked in the local paper-mill at Withnell Fold. On the outbreak of war he enlisted in the 7th (Service) Battalion King's Own.

He went overseas in July 1915 and saw action at Lens and Loos in the autumn before moving to the Somme in April 1916. The Battalion was in action at La Boiselle between 3 and 7 July and spent the end of July consolidating positions near Mametz Wood and Bazentin-le-Petit. Following the capture of enemy positions near the latter location on 30 July, Private Miller was ordered to take a message during a break in communications. The *London Gazette* of 9 September 1916 recorded the act of gallantry for which Private Miller was to receive a posthumous VC:

> For most conspicuous bravery. His battalion was consolidating a position after its capture by assault. Private Miller was ordered to take an important message under heavy shell and rifle fire, and to bring back a reply at all costs. He was compelled to cross the open, and on leaving the trench was shot almost immediately in the back, the bullet coming through his abdomen. In spite of this, with heroic courage and self-sacrifice, he compressed the gaping wound in his abdomen, delivered his message, staggered back with his answer, and fell dead at the feet of the officer to whom he delivered it. He gave his life with a supreme devotion to duty.

Private Miller is buried in Dartmoor Cemetery, near Becordel on the Somme. In his home village of Withnell a memorial in the form of a Celtic cross of Cornish granite was erected in 1917 by public subscription on the edge of the village churchyard; it was cleaned and restored in 1988. The Victoria Cross was presented to Private Miller's father by King George V at Buckingham Palace. Ellis Williams recorded Miller's gallantry in a contemporary poem entitled 'The Message'. His Victoria Cross was presented to the Regimental Museum by his family in September 1989.

18105 Private Jack White VC, 6th (Service) Battalion

Jack White was born Jacob Weiss on 23 December 1896 in Leeds, the son of a Russian Jewish immigrant father and British mother; the family subsequently moved to the Hightown district of Manchester. At the outbreak of war he was in Sweden, but returned, enlisted in the 6th (Service) Battalion King's Own and served throughout the war with the Battalion in the Middle East at Gallipoli and in Mesopotamia (Iraq). He was awarded the Victoria Cross for gallantry during an attempted crossing of the Dialah River by Captain S. Patterson and 60 men of the Battalion, including White, on the night of 7–8 March 1917. The award was published in the *London Gazette* of 27 June 1917:

> For most conspicuous bravery and resource. This signaller during an attempt to cross a river saw the two pontoons ahead of him come under heavy machine-gun fire, with disastrous results. When his own pontoon had reached mid-stream, with every man except himself either dead or wounded, finding that he was unable to control the pontoon Private White promptly tied a telephone wire to the pontoon, jumped overboard, and towed it to the shore, thereby saving the Officer's life and bringing to land the rifles and equipment of the other men in the boat, who were either dead or dying.

He returned home to a hero's welcome and was one of only five Jewish men to win the Victoria Cross up to 1939.

After the war he lived in Broughton, Salford, and worked in the textile business. He was also a founder member of the Jewish Ex-Servicemen's Association. In 1929 he attended the VCs' dinner at the House of Lords where he met Captain Patterson again for the first time since the war. At the outbreak of the Second World War he applied to join the Manchester Local Defence Volunteers (later Home Guard) but was rejected as his father had not been naturalised; the regulations were later changed, but he never forgot the slight. He served instead as a volunteer Air Raid Precaution worker. He died on 27 November 1949 aged 54 and was buried with full military honours in Blackley Jewish Cemetery near Manchester.

2950/200717 Lance-Sergeant Tom Fletcher Mayson VC, 1/4th Battalion (TF)

Tom Fletcher Mayson was born in December 1892 at Silecroft in Cumberland. He enlisted on 16 November 1914 in the 4th Battalion (TF) King's Own, served throughout the war on the Western Front and was wounded twice. He was awarded the Victoria Cross for gallantry at Wieltje in Belgium on 31 July 1917. The *London Gazette* published the citation on 14 September 1917:

> For most conspicuous bravery and devotion to duty when with the leading wave of the attack his

platoon was held up by machine-gun fire from a flank. Without waiting for orders, Lance-Sergeant Mayson at once made for the gun, which he put out of action with bombs, wounding four of the team. The remaining three of the team fled, pursued by Lance-Sergeant Mayson to a dugout into which he followed them, and disposed of them with his bayonet. Later when clearing up a strong point, this non-commissioned officer again tackled a machine-gun single-handed, killing six of the team. Finally, during an enemy counter-attack, he took charge of an isolated post, and successfully held it till ordered to withdraw as his ammunition was exhausted. He displayed throughout the most remarkable valour and initiative.

In December 1917 he received an enthusiastic welcome in Millom and his home village of Silecroft, where he was presented with a gold watch, chain, medal and illuminated address. He lived in Silecroft and worked at Sellafield until his death on 12 February 1958. He is buried in Whicham Churchyard, while his medals, less the original VC, are in the Regimental Museum.

241475 Private Albert Halton VC, 1st Battalion

Albert Halton was born on 1 May 1893 at Millhead, Warton, near Carnforth. He was educated in Carnforth, lived at 19 Highfield Terrace and was working for a local contractor when he enlisted in the 5th Battalion (TF) King's Own on 15 August 1915. He joined the 1/5th Battalion (TF) in France and was wounded on the Somme in October 1916; after recuperating in the UK he was posted to the 1st Battalion. He was awarded the Victoria Cross for gallantry during an attack near Poelcappelle on 12 October 1917. The *London Gazette* published the citation on 26 November 1917:

> For most conspicuous bravery in attack. After the objective had been reached Private Halton rushed forward about three hundred yards under very heavy rifle and shell-fire, and captured a machine-gun and its crew, which was causing many losses to our men. He then went out again and brought in about twelve prisoners, showing the greatest disregard of his own safety and setting a very fine example to those around him.

After the war Albert Halton worked for many years as a gateman at the Lansil Works in Lancaster until his retirement in 1961. He was a staunch supporter of the Regimental Association and attended most functions until his death on 24 July 1971. Towards the end of his life he lived at the Westfield War Memorial Village. Full military honours were provided for his funeral at Lancaster and Morecambe Crematorium.

2nd Lieutenant Joseph Henry Collin VC (Posthumous), 1/4th Battalion (TF)

Joseph Henry Collin was born on 11 March 1893 at Jarrow, Co Durham, and moved to Carlisle with his family when young. He lived at 8 Petteril Terrace, Harrowby, and was educated at St Patrick's School, where he was a keen athlete and footballer. At the outbreak of war he was working as an assistant at Hepworth's in Carlisle. In 1915 he enlisted in the Argyll and Sutherland Highlanders and served with them in France and Flanders. Promoted to Sergeant and later commissioned, he was posted as a Second Lieutenant to the 1/4th Battalion (TF) King's Own in France in October 1917. During the German Spring Offensive of 1918 he was awarded a posthumous Victoria Cross for bravery in defending a platoon position near Givenchy. The award was published in the *London Gazette* of 28 June 1918:

> For conspicuous bravery, devotion to duty, and self-sacrifice in action.
>
> After offering a long and gallant resistance against heavy odds in the 'Keep' held by his platoon, this officer, with only five of his men remaining, slowly withdrew in the face of superior numbers, contesting every inch of ground. The enemy was pressing him hard with bombs and machine-gun fire from close range. Single-handed 2/Lt Collin attacked the machine-gun team. After firing his revolver into the enemy, he seized a Mill's grenade and threw it into the hostile team, putting the gun out of action, killing four of the team, and wounding two others. Observing a second hostile machine-gun firing, he took a Lewis gun, and selecting a high point of vantage on the parapet whence he could engage the gun, he unaided kept the enemy at bay until he fell mortally wounded.
>
> The heroic self-sacrifice of 2/Lt Collin was a magnificent example to all.

Collin is buried in Vielle-Chapelle New Military Cemetery, France. His family presented a shield in his memory for a Mile Race to be completed for by Carlisle schools. They presented the Victoria Cross

to the Regimental Museum in 1971.

15883 Lance-Corporal James Hewitson VC, 1/4th Battalion (TF)

James Hewitson was born at Thwaite Farm, Coniston, on 5 October 1892. Educated at Coniston CE School, he enlisted in the 8th (Service) Battalion King's Own on 17 November 1914 and later transferred to the 1/4th Battalion (TF). Lance-Corporal Hewitson won his Victoria Cross near Givenchy on 26 April 1918 and was recommended on 8 May for the award, which was published in the *London Gazette* of 28 June 1918:

> For most conspicuous bravery, initiative and daring action. In a daylight attack on a series of crater posts L/Cpl Hewitson led his party to their objective with dash and vigour, clearing the enemy from both trench and dugouts, killing in one dugout six of the enemy who would not surrender. After capturing the final objective, he observed a hostile machine-gun team coming into action against his men. Working his way round the edge of the crater he attacked the team, killing four and capturing one. Shortly afterwards he engaged a hostile bombing party, which was attacking a Lewis gun post; he routed the party, killing six of them. The extraordinary feats of daring performed by this gallant non-commissioned officer crushed the hostile opposition at this point.

Promoted to Corporal, Hewitson received his VC from King George V in France on 8 August and returned home to a civic welcome in Coniston. Until his death, aged 74, on 2 March 1963, James Hewitson lived and worked in Coniston and is buried in the parish churchyard.

32827 Lance-Sergeant Tom Neely VC MM (Posthumous), 8th (Service) Battalion

Tom Neely was born on 28 March 1897 at Seacombe, near Wallasey in Cheshire, and was living in Liverpool when he joined the 8th (Service) Battalion King's Own. Having already won the Military Medal in 1918, he received the Victoria Cross for gallantry at Flesquieres on 27 September of that year. The *London Gazette* published the citation on 4 December 1918:

> For most conspicuous bravery during operations at Flesquieres on the 27th September 1918. His company was held up during the advance by heavy

machine-gun fire from a flank. Corporal Neely, realising the seriousness of the situation, at once, under point-blank fire, dashed out with two men and rushed the positions, disposing of the garrisons and capturing three machine-guns. Subsequently on two successive occasions he rushed concrete strong points, killing or capturing the occupants. The splendid initiative and fighting spirit displayed by this gallant non-commissioned officer in dealing with a series of posts, in some cases single-handed, was largely responsible for the taking and clearing of a heavily fortified and strongly garrisoned position, and enabled his company to advance 3,000 yards along the Hindenburg support line.

He was killed in action on 1 October 1918 near Rumilly and is buried in Masnieres Military Cemetery, France. His parents received his Victoria Cross from HM King George V at Buckingham Palace.

2nd Lieutenant Richard Leslie Brown GC, 1st Battalion

Richard Leslie Brown was born on 28 May 1898 in Huddersfield, West Yorkshire, and educated at Tydeswell School in Derbyshire. He was commissioned into the Regiment on 6 January 1917 and joined the 1st Battalion in France soon after. On 22 March 1917 the Battalion moved to Marquay (3 miles east of St Pol, 16 miles WNW of Arras) for training. The *London Gazette* of 4 January 1918 records:

> In France on 27th March 1917 Lt Brown was instructing a class on firing rifle grenades. Owing to a defective cartridge case one of the grenades was lifted only about two inches, and then fell back into the cup. The safety catch had been released and the grenade was fusing. Lt Brown at once ordered the men to clear and, running forward, picked up the rifle seizing it between his legs, grasped the grenade in his hand and endeavoured to throw it away. While he was doing so it exploded, blowing off his right hand, and inflicting other wounds. Had not Lt Brown seized the grenade in his hand, thus sheltering the men, there could be little doubt that several of them could have been killed or severely injured.

For this act of gallantry 2/Lt Brown was awarded the Albert Medal (2nd Class) For Saving Life on Land, which he received from HM King George V. As a predominantly civilian decoration, the award to 2/Lt Brown was unusual, particularly so as he was on active service. However, since his act of gallantry did not take place in contact with the enemy he received this award, unique to the Regiment, rather than a military decoration.

In 1971 HM Queen Elizabeth II decreed that all surviving holders of the Albert Medal would be invited to exchange them for a George Cross, and Mr Brown duly received his; his Albert Medal, at his request, was forwarded to the King's Own Regimental Museum by the Home Office.

After demobilisation in 1919 Mr Brown was employed as an engineer with Hopkinsons Ltd of Huddersfield. He subsequently became a Director of the company in 1928, Deputy Managing Director in 1929, Managing Director in 1933 and Chairman of the Board in 1942. In 1972 he finally retired and was appointed as the first Honorary President of Hopkinsons Holdings Limited in the following year. He retired to Annan in Dumfriesshire with his wife and was awarded the Queen's Silver Jubilee Medal in 1977; he died on 25 September 1982. Mr Brown's George Cross, War and Victory medals were acquired for the Regimental Museum in 1988.

Appendix 5

THE COLOURS OF THE REGIMENT

Colours of the Line/Regular Battalions

The Regiment received several stands of Colours during the early part of its existence, there being separate Colours for the Colonel, Lieutenant-Colonel, Major and each of the Companies; it is recorded that the Regiment took new Colours into use in 1680, 1687, 1702 and 1707. During the reigns of Queen Anne and George I, Regiments gradually abandoned the Company and Major's colours, retaining only the Colonel's and Lieutenant-Colonel's, which became the Regimental and King's or Queen's Colours.

The Colours carried in the late 18th and early 19th centuries measured 6 feet flying by 6 ft 6 in on a pike 9 ft 10 in long. By 1868 the size had been reduced to 3 ft 9 in by 3 feet on a pike 8 ft 7½ in long. The King's or Queen's Colour was the Union flag, to which ten Battle Honours were added after the First World War and a further ten after the Second. The last Queen's Colour of The King's Own Royal Regiment had in the centre the Regimental title within a circle. The Regimental Colour which, until 1881, had a small Union Flag in the top corner nearest the pike, was royal blue with a gold fringe. In the top corner nearest the pike was the Battalion number in Roman numerals, while in the centre was the Royal Cypher on a red ground within a circle inscribed with the Regimental title, all within a wreath of thistles, roses and shamrocks with a crown over. This was surrounded by sprays of laurel bearing the Regimental Battle Honours up to 1914 with, in each of the four corners, the Lion of England.

c1734– King's Own Regiment of Foot. Colonel's
1751 and Lieutenant-Colonel's Colours presented by William Barrell, probably when he became Colonel in 1734. Carried at Culloden. Passed eventually to the Stewarts of Ballachulish and through the Stewart Society laid up in the Scottish United Services Museum, Edinburgh Castle, on 1 August 1931.

1751 4th Regiment of Foot. New Colours taken into use. Date of replacement and location unknown.

1756 2nd Battalion 4th Foot. Passed to Colonel Alexander Duroure in 1758 and to his descendant Sir Godfrey Thomas. Returned to the Regiment in December 1946 and laid up in the Regimental Chapel on 17 August 1947.

1782 4th Foot. New Colours were imported to Ireland for the Regiment. In September 1797 they were thrown overboard on the voyage back from Canada to avoid capture by the French.

1799 1st Battalion 4th Foot. Presented by HRH the Prince of Wales on 3 September 1799. Carried in the Peninsula and at Waterloo. The King's Colour passed to Colonel Faunce, who gave it to Captain Mason in

1828. His daughter gave it to the Parish Church, Yateley, Hampshire, in September 1922. It was restored to the Regiment on 10 July 1927 and laid up in the Regimental Chapel on 8 November. Whereabouts of Regimental Colour unknown.

1799   2nd and 3rd Battalions 4th Foot raised in 1799 and disbanded in 1802. There is no record of Colours being presented to these Battalions.

1804   2nd Battalion 4th Foot. No record of the Colours. Battalion disbanded in December 1815.

1816   4th Foot. Presented by the Earl of Chatham at Fauquemberques, Pas-de-Calais, France. Location unknown.

1828   4th Foot. Presented by the Earl of Chatham at Glasgow on 27 September 1828. Passed to Sir Thomas Bradford in 1846 and deposited in Hartburn Parish Church, Northumberland, where they still hang.

1846   4th Foot. Presented by Lieutenant-Colonel Breton at Kampti, India, on 24 March 1846. Carried in the Crimea and during the Indian Mutiny. Placed in Exeter Guildhall in 1865, restored to the Regiment by Exeter Corporation on 17 May 1938, and laid up in the Regimental Chapel on 9 July.

1859   2nd Battalion 4th Foot. Presented by Sir James Yorke-Scarlett KCB at Chichester on 22 February 1859. Deposited in Windsor Castle on 13 December 1878. Restored to the Regiment on 9 July 1937 and laid up in the Regimental Chapel on 28 November.

1864   1st Battalion 4th Foot. Presented by Miss Frere at Poona, India, on 27 July 1864. Carried during the Abyssinian Campaign. Laid up in the Regimental Chapel on 23 February 1906.

1878   2nd Battalion 4th Foot. Presented by HM Queen Victoria at Windsor on 6 December 1878. These were the last Colours to be carried on active service, during the Zulu War. Laid up in the Regimental Chapel on 4 August 1926.

1905   1st Battalion King's Own. Presented by HRH the Prince of Wales at Fort William, Calcutta, on 30 December 1905. Laid up in the Regimental Chapel on 17 August 1947.

1926   2nd Battalion King's Own. Presented by Field Marshal Sir Claude Jacob GCB GCSI KCMG at Rawalpindi, India, on 27 January 1926. Retained by the 1st Battalion when the 2nd amalgamated with it on 22 April 1949. Laid up in the King's Chapel, Gibraltar, on 18 December 1955.

1947   1st Battalion King's Own. Presented by Major-General R. M. Luckcock CB CMG DSO at Trieste, Italy, on 25 July 1947. Laid up in the Regimental Chapel on 3 September 1961.

Colours of the Royal Lancashire Militia, Volunteer, Militia, Territorial and Service Battalions

1761   Royal Lancashire Militia. Presented by HM King George III on 15 October 1761. Carried in Ireland 1798/99. Hung in Colonel Stanley's London home until October 1816, when they were sent to Captain-Adjutant Wilkinson, Rose Cottage, Lancaster, for laying up in Lancaster Priory Church. Since then all trace has been lost.

1797   Loyal Lancaster Volunteers. King's Colour and 2nd Colour presented by the Town. Used until 1802 and then from 1803 to 1815. Passed to Colonel Whalley, whose daughter presented what remained of them to the Regimental Museum in 1931.

1801   Royal Lancashire Militia. Passed to Lieutenant-Colonel John Plumbe-Tempest and hung at his house, Tong Hall near Bradford. Only a portion of each colour remained. Whereabouts unknown.

1806   1st Royal Lancashire Militia. Presented by HM Queen Charlotte at Weymouth on 23 June 1806. Passed to Lieutenant-Colonel John Plumbe-Tempest who hung them at Tong Hall, near Bradford. Restored to the Regiment by his great-grand-daughter and laid up in the Regimental Chapel on 18 September 1932.

1804   Ulverston Volunteer Infantry. Presented by Lieutenant Colonel Thomas Sutherland, CO of Regiment, and given by his wife. Lodged in the Braddyl Chapel in October 1806, and hung in the Ulverston Drill Hall in 1873. Nothing remains of these Colours.

1816 1st Royal Lancashire Militia. Presented by the Lord Lieutenant of Ireland at Phoenix Park, Dublin. Given to Colonel John Plumbe-Tempest and hung at Tong Hall, Bradford. Restored to the Regiment (by Mrs Tempest) and laid up in the Regimental Chapel on 18 September 1932.

1853 1st Royal Lancashire Militia (Duke of Lancaster's Own). Presented by Mrs Clifton, wife of the Commanding Officer, at Giant Axe Field, Lancaster, 16 June 1853. Presented to Colonel Clifton in 1870 and hung at Lytham Hall. Regimental Colour given to the Regimental Museum by Guardian Estates, Lytham Hall, in 1972.

1870 1st Royal Lancashire Militia. Presented by Mrs Clifton at Lancaster on 27 June 1870. Carried by 1st Battalion when 1st Royal Lancashire Militia formed a 2nd Battalion in 1877 and later by the 3rd (Militia) Battalion King's Own. Laid up in the Regimental Chapel on 15 July 1905.

1880 2nd Battalion, 1st Royal Lancashire Militia. Presented by Lady Constance Stanley at Lancaster on 21 July 1880. Carried by 4th (Militia) Battalion King's Own and laid up in the Regimental Chapel on 15 July 1905.

1905 3rd (Militia) Battalion, King's Own. Presented by HM King Edward VII at Knowsley on 14 July 1905. Remained in use at the Regimental Depot until 1959. Laid up in the Regimental Chapel on 3 September 1961.

1905 4th (Militia) Battalion King's Own. Presented by HM King Edward VII at Knowsley on 14 July 1905. Deposited in Lancaster Town Hall when the Battalion disbanded in 1908. Laid up in the Regimental Chapel on 24 October 1928.

1909 4th (Territorial) Battalion King's Own. Presented by HM King Edward VII at Knowsley on 5 July 1909. Gift of Colonel Myles Kennedy. Carried by the Battalion and successor Artillery units until 1955. Laid up in Ulverston Parish Church on 24 April 1955.

1909 5th (Territorial) Battalion King's Own. Presented by HM King Edward VII at Knowsley on 5 July 1909. Gift of Lady Moira Cavendish. Refurbished in 1921 and laid up in the Regimental Chapel on 28 April 1963.

1919 2/5th (Territorial), 6th, 7th, 8th, 9th and 11th (Service) Battalions, King's Own. A King's Colour was issued for all these units, which were raised during the First World War. No details of presentation. Laid up in the Regimental Chapel in 1922.

1962 4/5th (Territorial) Battalion, King's Own. Presented by the Earl of Derby MC JP at Giant Axe Field, Lancaster, on 30 June 1962. Carried by the Battalion, its Cadre and 'E' Company Lancastrian Volunteers until 1975, when they were taken into use by the 4th (Volunteer) Battalion King's Own Royal Border Regiment (TAVR). Laid up in the Regimental Chapel on 13 July 1980.

Appendix 6

REGIMENTAL MARCHES AND MUSIC

Quick March — 'Corn Riggs are Bonnie'
This traditional North Country or Scottish air, composed *circa* 1680, was first used by the 2nd Battalion *circa* 1872 and officially adopted as the Regimental Quick March in 1881. The title and words were written by Robert Burns.

Prior to this the Regiment, like many others, marched past to 'The Lincolnshire Poacher'. 'Corn Riggs' is now incorporated in the Regimental Quick March of The King's Own Royal Border Regiment.

Slow March — 'And Shall Trelawny Die?'
It is not recorded when the Regiment adopted this march. Two members of the Trelawny family from the West Country, Charles and Henry, commanded and were successive Colonels of the Regiment from 1682 to 1702. Their brother Jonathan Trelawny was one of seven bishops imprisoned in the Tower by James II for petitioning against the Declaration of Indulgence. This caused such ill-feeling in the West Country that a song 'Shall Trelawny Die' was written. 'Trelawny' was adopted as the Slow March of The King's Own Royal Border Regiment in 1959.

Quick Step, 4th Regiment
Two bars of this march were discovered in a series of music books published *circa* 1800 by James Aird of Glasgow. Nothing more is known about it.

'Glorious First of August' (Glopriaug)
This was a ceremonial tune associated with a song celebrating the accession of George I on 1 August 1714. The song and tune were adopted by the Loyal and Friendly Society of the Blew and Orange, a society formed by Officers of the Regiment, *circa* 1733 as a mark of loyalty to the House of Hanover and in memory of William III.

'A Life on the Ocean Wave'
This was incorporated into the music of the Regiment in commemoration of its service as Marines from 1703 to 1710.

'Lancastria'
A Quick March composed by Bandmaster Thomas Chandler LRAM ARCM of the 2nd Battalion, 1918–35.

Appendix 7

REGIMENTAL ANNIVERSARIES AND REGIMENTAL COLLECT

St George's Day, 23 April

This day was traditionally celebrated by the Regiment because of its connection with William of Orange and the Royal Family. The earliest record of the Regiment participating in a parade on St George's Day is at Lisbon in 1704 and on Gibraltar in 1705, when it was serving as Marines. However, a formal St George's Day Parade is not recorded until 1898, when the 1st Battalion Trooped its Regimental Colour at Mount Austin Barracks in Hong Kong. The celebration in the Regular Battalions and at the Regimental Depot usually consisted of a formal parade where the Regimental Colour was trooped, followed by a sport's day or gymkhana and social gatherings such as a fancy dress ball. All ranks were presented with a red rose, which was worn in the head-dress, and a wreath of red roses was placed on each Colour; this practice is first recorded in 1908. The drums and Drum-Major's staff were also garlanded with roses.

Other Regimental Days and Anniversaries

When HM King Edward VII and HM George V were Colonels-in-Chief of the Regiment, the King's Birthday was celebrated. This occasionally took the form of a parade, when a 'feu de joie' was fired.

Prior to the First World War and between the wars, the Regiment commemorated various Battle Anniversaries, occasionally with a parade but usually with a display of Colours, social events and the playing of sports. Waterloo Day, 18 June, seems to have been the anniversary most regularly celebrated.

Regimental Collect

Lord Jesus, King of Glory, who dost love Thine own unto the end, grant, we pray Thee, that we, The King's Own Royal Regiment, may faithfully serve our Sovereign Lord the Queen, whose true soldiers we are; and in all our service may ever seek Thy Kingdom, who with the Father and the Holy Ghost livest and reignest for ever.

Appendix 8

NICKNAMES

Barrell's Blues

The Regiment was referred to by this title during and after the Colonelcy of General William Barrell (1734–49). 'Blues' refers to the blue facings worn by this, a Royal Regiment, since 1715. The practice of referring to Regiments by their Colonel's name was common until the mid-18th century. Barrell's name appears to have survived more prominently, probably due to the Regiment's gallant conduct at Culloden.

The Lions

From the Regiment's badge.

Appendix 9

ALLIED REGIMENT

The King's Own Calgary Regiment of Canada

The Calgary Regiment (Militia of Canada) was authorised after the First World War to succeed the 103rd Regiment (Calgary Rifles) and in recognition of the war service of the 50th Battalion Canadian Expeditionary Force in France and Flanders. HM King George V approved the Alliance with The King's Own Royal Regiment (Lancaster) on 5 September 1927. In 1931 past and present officers presented the Calgary Regiment with a Lion centrepiece.

During the Second World War the Regiment was redesignated as The (Calgary Regiment) 14th Canadian Armoured Regiment. It served with distinction at Dieppe in 1942, throughout the campaigns in Sicily, Italy and Holland, and in Germany in 1945. After the war, 'King's Own' was added to the Regiment's title and it became known as The King's Own Calgary Regiment. In 1953 HM Queen Elizabeth II became the Regiment's Colonel-in-Chief. This Alliance has been maintained by The King's Own Royal Border Regiment.

INDEX

BIBLIOGRAPHY

Published sources of the Regiment
Cannon, R. *Historical Record of the Fourth or King's Own Regiment of Foot* (London, 1839)
Coop, J. O. *The Story of the 55th (West Lancashire) Division* (Liverpool, 1919)
Cowper, L. I. *The King's Own — The Story of a Royal Regiment,* Volumes 1 and 2, 1680-1914 (Oxford, 1939)
Cowper, J. M. *The King's Own — The Story of a Royal Regiment,* Volume 3, 1914-1950 (Aldershot and London, 1957)
Fell, A. *A Furness Military Chronicle* (Ulverston, 1937)
Foley, J. *Mailed Fist* (St Albans, 1975)
Green, H. *The King's Own* (Famous Regiments Series, London, 1972)
HMSO *Soldiers Died in the Great War, Part 9 — The King's Own Royal Lancaster Regt* (London, 1921)
Hodgkinson, A. *History of the 1/5th Battalion King's Own Royal Lancashire Regiment in the European War 1914-1918* (Lewes, 1921)
The Lion and The Rose, 1905-1959
The Lion and The Dragon, 1960-1991
May, R. K. *A Short History of the King's Own Royal Border Regiment 1680-1980*
Rawsthorne, J. G. *An Account of the Regiments of Royal Lancashire Militia 1759-1870* (Lancaster, 1874)
Sutherland, D. C. H. *Tried and Valiant — The Story of the Border Regiment 1702-1959* (London, 1972)
Wadham, W. F. A. and Crossley, J. *The Fourth Battalion The King's Own (Royal Lancaster Regiment) and The Great War* (Ulverston, 1935)
Williams, E. *Ballads of The King's Own and Other Verses* (Lancaster, 1918)
Williamson, R. J. T. and Whalley, J. Lawson *Historical Records of the 1st Royal Lancashire Militia* (London, 1888)
History of 107th Regiment Royal Armoured Corps (King's Own) (Lengerich, W Germany, 1946)
A History of 34th Independent Armoured Brigade

Unpublished sources — held in the Regimental Museum Archives
Digest of Services, 1st and 2nd Battalions, 1680-1939
Digest of Service, 1st Royal Lancashire Militia, 3rd and 4th Militia Battalions King's Own Royal Lancaster Regiment, 1852-1914
War Diaries, 1st, 2nd, 1/4th, 1/5th, 2/5th, 6th, 7th, 8th, 9th, 11th Battalions, 1914-1919
War Diary, 2nd Battalion, 1939-1945
Bois, J. A. *A Historical Record of the 2nd Battalion 1914-1919*
Keith, G. T. E. *A History of the King's Own 1680-1914*
Keith, G. T. E. *Officers List King's Own Royal Regiment (Lancaster) 1680-1959*
The Letters of Lieutenant H. C. Borrett written during the Abyssinian Campaign, 1868
Miller, Rev W. H. *Diary of a Chaplain — Chindit Campaign 1944*
Numerous unpublished accounts, letters and other documentary material in the Regimental Archives held in Lancaster City Museum.

Periodicals
Journal of the Society for Army Historical Research, 1922-1991
The Bulletin — The Journal of the Military Historical Society
Navy and Army Illustrated

Other published sources
Allinson, S. *The Bantams — The Untold Story of WW1* (London, 1981)
Army Museums, Ogilby Trust *Index to British Military Costume Prints 1500-1914* (London, 1972)
Ascoli, D. *The Mons Star — The British Expeditionary Force 1914* (London, 1984)
Atkin, R. *Pillar of Fire — Dunkirk 1940* (London, 1990)
Bancroft, J. W. *Devotion to Duty* (Manchester, 1990)
Barthorp, M. *British Army Uniforms Since 1660* (Dorset, 1982)
Barthorp, M. *Crimean Uniforms — British Infantry* (London, 1974)
Bidwell, S. *The Chindit War* (London, 1979)
Brereton, J. M. *The British Soldier — A Social History from 1661 to the present day* (London, 1986)
Carmen, W. Y. and Simkins, R. *Uniforms of the British Army — The Infantry Regiments* (Exeter, 1985)
Cohen, J. *Journey to the Trenches — The Life of Isaac Rosenberg 1890-1918* (London, 1975)
Glover, R. *The Peninsular War* (Newton Abbot and London, 1974)
Gordon, L. L. *British Battles and Medals* (London, 1979)
Griffiths, K. *Thank God We Kept the Flag Flying — The Siege and Relief of Ladysmith 1899-1900* (New York, 1975)
Guedalia, P. *The Middle East — A Study in Air Power* (London, 1944)
Hastings, M. *Overlord — D-Day and the Battle for Normandy 1944* (London, 1984)
Hibbert, C. *Corunna* (London, 1967)
MacKenzie, B. S. *Loyally They Served — A Short History of the Queen's Lancashire Regiment 1689-1970*
Masters, J. *The Road Past Mandalay* (London, 1961)
Middlebrook, M. *The First Day on The Somme* (London, 1970)
Mollo, B. *The British Army from Old Photographs* (London, 1975)
Moore, W. *See How They Ran* (London, 1970)
Morris, D. *The Washing of The Spears* (London, 1972)
Myatt, F. *The March to Magdala* (London, 1970)
Myatt, F. *The British Infantry 1660-1945 — The Evolution of a Fighting Force* (Poole, 1985)
Nicholson, J. B. R. *British Army of the Crimea* (Reading, 1974)
Oman, C. *Sir John Moore* (London, 1953)
Packenham, T. *The Boer War* (London, 1979)
Prebble, J. *Culloden* (London, 1988)
Reilly, R. *The British at the Gates — The New Orleans Campaign in the War of 1812* (London, 1976)
Terraine, J. *Mons — The Retreat to Victory* (London, 1972)
This England, The Register of the Victoria Cross
Warner, P. *Army Life in the 1890s* (London, 1975)
Westlake, R. *Kitchener's Army — A Pictorial History 1914-1918* (Tunbridge, 1989)
Westlake, R. *The Territorial Battalions — A Pictorial History 1859-1985* (London, 1986)
Wylly, H. C. *The Loyal North Lancashire Regiment,* Volume 1 (London, 1933)